COURAGE TO PRAY

Courage to Pray

METROPOLITAN ANTHONY
and
GEORGES LEFEBVRE OSB

Translated by
Dinah Livingstone

Darton, Longman and Todd
London

St Vladimir's Seminary Press
Crestwood, New York 10707
1984

First published in 1973 by
Darton, Longman and Todd Ltd
89 Lillie Road, London SW6 1UD

Originally published in France as
La Prière by Maison Mame, Paris
This translation © 1973 by Darton, Longman & Todd Ltd

Sixth impression 1981

This edition published 1984
together with
St. Vladimir's Seminary Press
575 Scarsdale Road
Crestwood, New York 10707

ISBN 0 232 51612 X (DLT)
ISBN 0-88141-031-4 (SVS Press)

Printed and bound in Great Britain by
Anchor Brendon Ltd
Tiptree, Essex

Part I

Courage to Pray

by

Metropolitan Anthony

CONTENTS

A DISCOVERY

PRAYER IS THE search for God, encounter with God, and going beyond this encounter in communion. Thus it is an activity, a state and also a situation; a situation both with respect to God and to the created world. It arises from the awareness that the world in which we live is not simply two dimensional, imprisoned in the categories of time and space, a flat world in which we meet only the surface of things, an opaque surface covering emptiness. Prayer is born of the discovery that the world has depths; that we are not only surrounded by visible things but that we are also immersed in and penetrated by invisible things. And this invisible world is both the presence of God, the supreme, sublime reality, and our own deepest truth. Visible and invisible are not in opposition neither can they be juxtaposed like in an addition sum. They are present simultaneously, as fire is present in red hot iron. They complete each other in a mysterious way which the English writer Charles Williams describes as 'co-inherence': the presence of eternity in time and the future in the present, and also the presence of each temporal moment in eternity, past present and future all-at-once eschatologically, the one in the other as the tree is in the seed. Living only in the visible world is living on the surface; it ignores or sets

aside not only the existence of God but the depths of
created being. It is condemning ourselves to perceiving
only the world's surface. But if we look deeper we discover at the heart of things a point of balance which is
their finality. There is no inwardness to geometric
volume. Its finiteness is complete. The world of such
forms is capable of being extended but cannot be
deepened. But the heart of man is deep. When we have
reached the fountainhead of life in him we discover
that this itself springs from beyond. The heart of man
is open to the invisible. Not the invisible of depth
psychology but the invisible infinite, God's creative word,
God himself. Returning to ourselves is thus not a
synonym for introversion but for emerging beyond the
limits of our limited selves. Saint John Chrysostom said
'When you discover the door of your heart you discover
the gate of heaven.' This discovery of our own depths
goes together with the recognition of the depths in
others. Each has his own immensity. I use the word
'immensity' on purpose. It means that the depth cannot be measured, not because it is too great for our
measurements to reach it, but because its quality is
not subject to measurement at all. The immensity of
our vocation is to share the divine nature, and in discovering our own depths we discover God, whom we
could call our invisible neighbour, the Spirit, Christ, the
Father. We also discover God's immensity and eternity
in the world about us. And this is the beginning of
prayer, the recognition of a three-dimensional world
of time, space and a stable but ever changing depth.

A TRIPLE RELATIONSHIP

Prayer is the relationship between man the visible and
the invisible x. This is why I said that prayer is a search,
an exploration of this invisible world of our own depths
which God alone knows and he alone can reveal to us.

And it is by prayer, gropingly at first, in the dawn of a new vision, that we seek and find God and ourselves in a co-relative way. Then later, when a clearer light has shown us what we can see of the invisible and the visible transfigured in the light of its own immensity and the eternity in God, prayer becomes a state. It also constantly remains a situation, as I said at the beginning. While we are seeking, part blind with partly restored sight, our first steps in prayer take the form of astonishment, reverent fear and a sense of sadness. We are astonished at the discovery of ourselves which is also the beginnings of knowledge of God; we are astonished to see the world open out towards God's infinity. We are afraid, glad and terrified when we come into the presence of God's holiness and beauty. We are also sad, both for ourselves and the world. It is sad to be blind, it is sad to be unable to live the fulness of our vocation, to be trapped again and again in our own limitations. It is sad to see our world without God, vacillating between life and death and unable to choose life once and for all or to escape once and for all from death. Wonder and sadness are thus the two sources of our prayer. Both arise from our encounter with the world's depths, which have begun to be revealed to us in their totality. Without this encounter, our world and the forces at work in it are incomprehensible and often monstrous; we are bewildered and afraid.

ENCOUNTER

Thus encounter is central to prayer. It is the basic category of revelation, because revelation itself is an encounter with God who gives us a new vision of the world. Everything is encounter, in scripture as in life. It is both personal and universal, unique and exemplary. It always has two poles: encounter with God and in him with creation, an encounter with man in his depths rooted in God's creative will, straining towards fulfil-

ment when God will be all in all. This encounter is personal because each of us must experience it for himself,
we cannot have it second-hand. It is our own, but it also
has a universal significance because it goes beyond our
superficial and limited ego. This encounter is unique because for God as for one another when we truly see,
each of us is irreplaceable and unique. Each creature
knows God in his own way. Each one of us knows God in
our own way which no one else will ever know unless
we tell them. And at the same time because human
nature is universal, each encounter is exemplary. It is a
revelation to all of what is known personally by each.

AS THROUGH A GLASS DARKLY

We should try and analyse this encounter carefully, because if we do not know the laws it follows we may let it
slip away. It is always a mutual encounter. It is always
a discovery not only of the other but of ourselves. It is
always a relationship. Perhaps the best image for it is a
stained glass window. The light shining through it shows
up its design, its colours, its beauty and its meaning. But
at the same time the window itself by its design,
colours, beauty and meaning reveals for us the invisible
light beyond it. Thus the window and the light are discovered in relationship to one another. Discovering God
in his serene eternity and in the man of sorrows who was
the incarnate word, is also a discovery of the greatness of
man. When we discover the depths in man, we go
beyond the front he presents to us and discover his
destiny which is not individual but personal. This destiny
makes him more than an example of humankind; it
makes him the member of a mysterious body, the whole
of mankind, which is where God's presence is.

THE NATURE OF THIS ENCOUNTER

However at the start any man seeking this encounter is

alone and must learn to recognise the existence of the other. And this recognition must take place in a relationship and not in isolation. This is important. We know nothing and nobody except through a relationship. If we are disconnected nothing exists for us. But there is a danger in not knowing anything or anybody except in relation to ourselves. This is to de-centre the universe. In referring everything to ourselves we deform it and make it as small and mean as we are, with our small mean cravings. So when we begin to recognise the existence of the other, we must be prepared to set ourselves aside to some extent, to go beyond ourselves and to admit the other's needs and his rights to independence and freedom, outside us. We must accept his irreducible *otherness*. Whatever we do, however well we know him, however close we are, and this is even truer of man and God than man and man, there remains a central mystery which we can never solve. In the Book of Revelation there is the marvellous passage where John says that those who go into the Kingdom are given a white stone with a name written on it which only they and God know. This name is not the label we are given and called by in this world. Our true name, our eternal name exactly fits us, our whole being ... It defines and expresses us perfectly. It is known by God alone and he tells us what it is. No one else can know it because it expresses our unique relationship with our creator. How often human relationships come to grief because one person wants to reveal himself beyond what is possible or the other person wants to probe into a territory which is sacred to God alone. It is a vain wish and cannot be fulfilled. It is like a child trying to find the source of a spring, the point where the water begins, that point just before which there is no water. In this case it is only possible to destroy, not to discover.

But it is not enough to recognise the other's right to

exist, to accept his irreducible otherness. We must be able to see, hear and judge. Otherwise the encounter cannot be fruitful.

SEEING

Christ speaks of the clear vision we need to see things as they are. If there is something wrong with our eyes we project shadows onto things or see instead the distorted shapes which our poor eyes form in our imagination. But clear vision is not enough. We must choose the right standpoint. We must find the right distance, from which we can see an object whole. Isn't this essential when we are looking at a work of art? A painting or a statue needs to be seen from not too close and not too far away. There is the best standpoint, from which we see it as the artist intended, from which we can see the whole and are not overwhelmed by its parts. The same is true of human relationships. We must find the right distance, not in time and space but in inner freedom; freedom which is a bond but not a chain.

An example I have used in a previous book will perhaps make the point better than a long discussion. In a remarkable book the English author Charles Williams shows us a girl who has just been killed in a plane crash. Her soul released from her body discovers a new world which she never saw before, she has just entered the invisible world which is now the only reality to her. She cannot see the visible world with the eyes of her soul. At one point she finds herself beside the Thames. She had seen it before as a foul stretch of filthy water, a refuse dump for London. But because she is now out of her body and does not relate everything to herself, she *sees* the Thames for the first time. She discovers it as a fact, a great river flowing through a great city. Its waters are dirty and opaque, they carry London's refuse to the sea. But this is as it should be, this is their proper role and they are authentic. And when she sees them as they are and accepts them, without emotion or physical repulsion because she can no longer feel disgust for them no longer having a body, to bathe in them or lips to drink from them, she sees the depths of the waters. They become less and less opaque. And at last they become transparent. This transparency increases until at the heart of the waters she sees a luminous thread which is the primordial water, as God created it, and at the heart of this primordial water, a yet more luminous thread, which is the marvellous water that Christ offered the Samaritan woman.

Through her disembodiment, the dead girl has been able to see things she was formerly blind to. The same is true of us. If we could become detached from ourselves and gain the inner freedom which the Fathers called 'apathy', that is to say the absence of passion, we could see things more and more luminously. We could also see the splendour of God's presence in this dark and opaque world. We could see grace active everywhere and in all things.

HEARING

I said before that seeing is not enough. We must also hear. Hearing is an act of sustained attention. In order to hear, we must not only lend our ears, but also try and understand the meaning and intention of the words. Hearing means bowing our heads in humility which is capable of accepting what the other person is sowing on the ground of our mind and heart. This is the true meaning of the word 'humility'. The word comes from the Latin 'humus', fertile soil, that soil which we no longer notice because we are so used to it, dumb and dark, capable of making good use of the rubbish we tip onto it, capable of transforming our refuse into wealth, of accepting every seed, giving it body, life, growth, to become fully itself, without ever denaturing it. Our own power of hearing begins with humility. Like the rich silent, creative earth, we should offer ourselves to the Other.

HUMILITY AND OBEDIENCE

But this humility is also obedience. The Latin word *obaudire* means both to listen and obey. We must listen in order to hear and profit by what we hear. This is the proper attitude to God, total attention because we must hear him, and the desire, determination to receive his message and profit by it, that is to say be transformed, changed, to stop being what we are and become what we are called to be. This fundamental attitude of prayer is a bit like a bird watcher. He gets up early in the morning because he must reach the fields and woods before the birds wake up, so that they will not see him coming. He is silent and keeps quite still. He is all eyes and ears. He is receptive to every sound and every movement. He listens and he watches but he will not see what is happening around him unless he is free of prejudices, ready to hear what God speaks. It is an attitude of self surrender which is at the same time extremely active. Self surrender because like the earth, *humus* he offers himself without reserve. Active because he is ready to respond to God's every suggestion, every call. It follows that if we want to have a real encounter with God, we need more than mere organs of hearing and vision. We must have the enthusiasm, the desire, we must want to hear and see.

OBEDIENCE AND LOVE

And for this we must love. However little, we must love. Charles Williams in the same book *All Hallows Eve* which I quoted above, describes on the first page the soul of his dead heroine on one of the bridges of London where she died. She sees nothing but herself, the point at which her feet touch the ground and the aeroplane which crashed and killed her. She sees nothing because her heart is attached to nothing. She sees an empty bridge when in fact it is crowded with pedestrians, all the time. On either bank of the Thames she sees houses, but as walls with gloomy eyes, windows which light up and go dark again but meaninglessly. She has no key to the world around her because she has never loved anything and is a stranger here. Suddenly her husband, now her widower walks over the bridge. They see each other, he because he loves her and he bears her in his heart, weeps for her and seeks her in the invisible world, she because he is the only person she ever loved in her poor selfish way. He is the only person she can see. She sees him. He goes on. But her heart has stirred and through her husband she remembers her world, husband, their home and friends. And gradually, through this love she begins to discover the world she lived in without knowing it and at the same time the new vast world she has just entered. These two worlds interpenetrate in the co-inherence which is Charles Williams particular philosophical theory. For we only see what we love. We think we see what we hate, but really in our hatred we see only deformed images, caricatures. And indifference and lukewarmness are blind.

AN EYE PURIFIED TO JUDGE

But to know truly, to see reality in an adequate manner, it is not enough to look, listen or even to love. We must also have a pure heart capable of finding God beyond the darkness which hides him. Just as an unclear eye projects its own shadow on all it sees, so an impure heart cannot judge or see things in the way that God sees them.

A story about the desert fathers illustrates this clearly. One of them followed by his disciples comes to the gates

of Alexandria. He sees a very beautiful woman coming
along the road. The disciples cover their heads with their
cloaks so as not to fall into temptation. Perhaps they
escape from the temptation of the flesh, but not from the
temptation of curiosity. From underneath their cloaks
they see their master and are scandalised to find that he
is looking straight at the approaching woman. After she
has gone into the town, they remove their cloaks and
ask him, 'How could you succumb to the temptation
to look at this woman?' He replied sadly, 'How impure
are your hearts. You saw her only as a temptation. I saw
her as one of God's wonders.'

THE EXPERIENCE OF A STARETZ

So every encounter with God or man has more than
technical requirements. When we seek God we must love
our neighbours and when we seek our neighbours we
must love God. In one of his letters a Russian *staretz*
describes how one day he was asked a question: 'Why is
it that the workers under your charge work so hard and
so well when you do not watch over them and those that
we watch over are always trying to deceive us.' The holy
man replied: 'When I come in the morning to give them
their work, I am overcome with pity for them. They have
left their village and their family for a tiny wage, how
poor they must be. And when I have given them their
work I go back into my cell and pray for each one of
them I say to the Lord: "Lord, remember Nicholas
he is so young, he has left his new-born child to find
work because they are so poor he has no other means
of supporting it. Think of him and protect him from evil
thoughts. Think of her and be her defender." Thus I pray
but as I feel the presence of God more and more strongly,
I reach a point when I can no longer take notice of anything on earth. The earth vanishes, God alone remains.
Then I forget Nicholas, his wife, his child, his village, his

poverty and am carried away in God. Then deep in God I find the divine love which contains Nicholas, his wife, his child, their poverty, their needs and this divine love is a torrent which carries me back to earth and to praying for them. And the same thing happens again. God's presence becomes stronger, earth recedes. I am carried again into the depths where I find the world that God so greatly loves.' Encounter with God, encounter with man. They are only possible when both are so greatly loved that the one who prays can forget himself, become detached from himself, and become only an 'orientation' towards them, for them. This the fundamental character of intercession.

I should now like to explore this theme of encounter a bit further. First I should like to stress that encounter with God and man is *dangerous*. It is not without reason that the eastern tradition of Zen calls the place where we find him whom we seek the tiger's lair. Seeking God is an act of boldness, unless it is an act of complete humility. Encountering God is always a *crisis* and the Greek word crisis means *judgment*. This encounter can take place in wonder and humility. It can also take place in terror and condemnation. So it is not surprising that orthodox manuals on prayer give very little space to questions of technique and method but endless advice on the necessary moral and spiritual conditions for prayer. Let us recall some of these. First the gospel commandment: 'If you come to the temple and you remember that your brother has something against you, leave your gift, return to him you have offended and make your peace with him, then come back and offer your gift'. This commandment is taken up in an excellent manner by Simeon the New Theologian, who tells us that if we want to pray with a free heart, we must make our peace with God, our conscience, our neighbour and even the things about us. That is to say that the condition of a life

of prayer is a life in accordance with the gospel. A life
which makes the commandments and counsels given us
by the gospel second nature.

It is not enough to obey them as a slave obeys his
master's will. We must want to obey with all our heart,
like a son, like children of the kingdom who truly want
what they pray when they say 'Hallowed be thy name,
thy kingdom come, thy will be done'.

Let us now consider an encounter with the Lord in a
number of particular situations, in humility, in truth, in
despair, in tumult, in life, in silence, in the liturgy.

IT IS TERRIBLE TO FALL INTO THE HANDS
OF THE LIVING GOD

If we remembered that every encounter with God and
every deep encounter with man is a judgment, a crisis,
we would seek God both more whole-heartedly and more
cautiously. We would not be bitter if this encounter did
not immediately take place. We would approach God
with a trembling heart. In this way we would avoid many
disappointments, many useless efforts, because God
would not give himself to us if we could not bear the
encounter. He prepares us for it, and sometimes by a
long wait. The Gospel gives us examples of the attitude
we should imitate. Luke shows us ten lepers seeking to
be cured. They come towards Christ and stop a little
way off because they know they are impure. And in their
misery they cry to the Lord with all the faith and hope
they are capable of but without going up to him. And
the Lord does not take one step towards them. He simply
commands them to go and show themselves to the
priests. He promises them nothing. He sends them to
their cure. And this cure is granted them in their faith,
hope and humble obedience. How different is their
humility from our prayer of 'humble access' when we
should be trembling but are often arrogant.

We may also remember the example of St Peter who realised his master's godhead through his words and the miraculous draught of fishes, and fell at his feet crying, 'depart from me for I am a sinful man, O Lord'. The vision of the holiness and glory of God did not lead him to seek an intimacy with it which he could not bear. He asked the Lord to go away. But the Lord decided to stay.

We have also in the gospel the story of the centurion who asks the Lord to cure his servant and when the Lord says he will come, the centurion replies, 'Lord I am not worthy that you should enter under my roof, say but the word.' A total faith and perfect trust, such great humility which should shame us because we do not feel our own sinfulness enough, we do not feel ourselves unworthy enough to ask the Lord not to trouble himself at the same time believing that he can do everything for us.

But this is a basic attitude. Unless we give up seeking a tangible shining presence of the Lord, we are going towards our own judgment. If the Lord comes to us, we should receive him with great joy and humility. But let us be careful not to seek mystical experience when we should be seeking repentance and conversion. That is the beginning of our cry to God. 'Lord make me what I should be, change me whatever the cost.' And when we have said these dangerous words, we should be prepared for God to hear them. And these words of God are dangerous because God's love is remorseless. God wants our salvation with the determination due to its importance. And God, as the Shepherd of Hermas says 'does not leave us till he has broken our heart and bones'.

LET ME KNOW MYSELF

A second form of encounter is the encounter in the truth. An encounter is only true when the two persons meeting are true. And from this point of view, we are

continually falsifying this encounter. Not only in ourselves but in our image of God, it is very difficult for us
to be true. Throughout the day we are a succession of
social personalities, sometimes unrecognisable to others
or even to ourselves. And when the time comes to pray
and we want to present ourselves to God we often feel
lost because we do not know which of these social personalities is the true human person, and have no sense
of our own true identity. The several successive persons
that we present to God are not ourselves. There is something of us in each of them but the whole person is
missing. And that is why a prayer which could rise
powerfully from the heart of the true person cannot find
its way between the successive men of straw we offer to
God. Each of these speaks a word which is true in its
own partial way, but does not express the other partial
personalities we have been during the day. It is extremely
important that we find our unity, our fundamental
identity. Otherwise we cannot encounter the Lord in
truth. The search for this unity may take time. We should
be on the watch all the time to see that none of our
words and actions are incompatible with the fundamental integrity we are seeking. We must try and discover
the real person we are, the secret person, the core of the
person to come and the only eternal reality which is
already in us. This discovery is difficult because we have
to cast aside all the men of straw. From time to time
something authentic shows through, when we forget ourselves our deep reality may take over, in moments when
we are carried away by joy so that we forget who might
be looking at us, forget to stand aside and look at ourselves, or when we are unselfconscious in moments of
extreme pain, moments when we have a deep sense of
sadness or of wonder. At these moments we see something of the true person that we are. But no sooner have
we seen, than we often turn away because we do not

want to confront this person face to face. We are afraid
of him, he puts us off.

Nevertheless this is the only real person there is in
us. And God can save this person, however repellent he
may be, because it is a true person. God cannot save the
imaginary person that we try to present to him, or to
others or ourselves. As well as seeking the real person in
us, through these chance manifestations, we must also
seek constantly the person we are to God. We must seek
for God in us and ourselves in God. This is a work of
meditation which we should engage in every day all
through our lives.

We can begin simply. When we read the scriptures
honestly we can admit that certain passages mean little
to us. We are ready to agree with God because we have
no reason to disagree with him. We can approve of this
or that commandment or divine action because it does
not touch us personally, we do not yet see the demands
it makes on us personally. Other passages frankly,
repel us. If we had the courage we would say 'no' to the
Lord. We should note these passages carefully. They are
a measure of the distance between God and us and also,
perhaps more importantly for our present point, they are
a measure of the distance between ourselves as we are
now and our potential definitive selves. For the gospel is
not a succession of external commandments, it is a whole
gallery of internal portraits. And every time we say 'no'
to the Gospel we are refusing to be a person in the full
sense of the word.

There are also passages of the gospel which make our
hearts burn, which give light to our intelligence and
shake up our will. They give life and strength to our
whole physical and moral being. These passages reveal
the points where God and his image in us already co-
incide, the stage we have already reached, perhaps only
momentarily, fleetingly, in becoming what we are called

to be. We should note these passages even more carefully than the passages mentioned above. They are the
points at which God's image is already present in us
fallen men. And from these beginnings we can strive to
continue our transformation into the person we feel we
want and ought to be. We must be faithful to these
revelations. In this at least we must always be faithful.
If we do this these passages increase in number, the
demands of the gospel become fuller and more precise,
slowly the fogs disperse and we see the image of the
person we should be. Then we can begin standing before
God in truth. However as well as this essential, fundamental truth, there is also the partial truth of the
moment.

How often our prayer is false because we try to present
ourselves to God not as we are, but as we imagine he
wants us to be. We come to him in our Sunday best or
in borrowed finery. It is important that before we start
to pray we should take time to recollect ourselves, to
reflect and become aware of the real state in which we
present ourselves to the Lord. 'My heart is ready, Lord.
my heart is ready,' we can say. 'As pants the hart for
cooling streams, so longs my soul for Thee O God.' But
too often we drag ourselves into God's presence by a
dour effort of will. We are doing a duty with no heart
in it. We force ourselves to appear to be what we know
we are deep down but do not at the moment feel. The
living waters have sunk in dry sands. We should tell
this to God who is the truth. 'Lord I come to you with a
dry heart, but I am forcing myself to stand before you
because of a deep conviction. I love and worship you with
my deepest being, but today this deepest being has failed
to surface.' Sometimes we find that we do not even
present ourselves to God out of deep conviction, but out
of an almost superstitious fear. 'If I do not pray perhaps
God will withdraw his protection from me.' We should

confess this distrust and lack of faith and hope in God's
love and faithfulness. There are many other ways in
which we present ourselves to God. We have to become
aware of these different states in which we pray. Otherwise our prayer will not even contain the truth of the
moment. It will be an absolute lie, a betrayal of both
the old and the new Adam in us. It will neither be true
to what is stable and eternal in us nor to passing
moods.

LET ME KNOW YOU

But an encounter does not depend on the truth of only
one of the parties to it. The Other is equally important.
The God we encounter must be as true as we who seek
him. But is not God always true? Is he not always himself, unchanging? Of course. But it is not only God as he
is in himself who is involved in our prayers. It is also the
image we have of him, for our attitude depends not only
on what he is in himself but also on what we believe
him to be. If we have a false image of God, our attitude
towards him and our prayer will alter accordingly. It is
important that throughout our life, from day to day we
learn to know God as he is. Not in the fragmented way
which makes us see him sometimes as a ruthless
judge and sometimes as a loving saviour, but in all his
complexity. We must also beware of thinking that even
the sum total of human knowledge of God constitutes
an authentic image of the living God. God, even as he
reveals himself in scripture, does not reveal himself in a
total and final manner. If we try and place ourselves
before an image of God made up of all that we know of
him through revelation, through the experience of the
church, our own experience, we are in danger of standing before a false image, because it pretends to be a
total image, when it can only ever be a poor approxi-
mation. As Gregory of Nazianzus says, this is worship-

ping an idol. This is why the Eastern Church Fathers
continually stress the necessity of presenting ourselves
to God without images or imaginings of him. Everything
that we know about God should lead us to God, but when
we stand before him, we should leave all this knowledge
of him behind, however true and rich it may be. We
should stand before the unknown God, the mystery, the
divine darkness, we should be ready to meet God as he
wishes to reveal himself to us today. Otherwise it will
always be the God of yesterday, and not the true God
himself. But the true God is the only object of our seeking, the only partner in authentic prayer. This encounter
in the truth cannot happen with an artificial presence,
because in our encounter we are not seeking merely
emotions of joy, ecstasy etc. but God himself.

THE ABSENCE OF GOD

And in this context of truth we must recognise the fact
that God may be absent. This absence is of course sub-
jective, in so far as God is always present to us. But he
may remain invisible and intangible. He escapes us.
What we said above about humility should help us here.
When God does not give himself to us, when we cannot
feel his presence, we must be able to wait with awe and
reverence. But there is also another element in this sub-
jective absence of God. A relationship can only be true
if it takes place in mutual freedom. We too often feel
that we have only to start praying for God to be obliged
to offer himself to us, to listen to us, to let us feel his
presence, to assure us that he hears us. If this were so, it
would not be a free relationship, it would be mechanical
and could have no joy and spontaneity. It would also
suppose that we were always in a fit state to see God.
Alphonse de Chateaubriand in a remarkable book on
prayer called *La Réponse du Seigneur*, tells us that God's
apparent absence is usually caused by our own blindness.

I should like to illustrate this phrase by an example.

One day a man came to see me, a man who had been searching for God for many years. He told me in tears: 'Father I cannot live without God. Show me God.' I told him that I was unable to show him God, but I did not think that he was in a fit state to see him anyway. Astonished, he asked me why. Then I asked him a question which I often ask those who come to see me. 'Is there a passage in the scripture which goes straight to your heart, the most precious passage you have found?' 'Yes,' he replied, 'the story of the adulterous woman in John chapter eight.' Then I asked him, 'Where do you see yourself in this scene?' Are you the woman who has become conscious of her sin and stands to be judged, knowing that it will be a judgment of life or death? Or do you identify with Christ who understands everything and will forgive her, so that she can live with a new life henceforth? Are you waiting for a reply and hoping it will be merciful, as the apostles must have been? Are you one of the crowd, one of the old men who knew they had sinned themselves and were the first to withdraw, or one of the young men who gradually realised they too were sinners and dropped the stones they had picked up to throw? Who are you in this dramatic scene? And after a moment's reflection this man replied, 'I am the only Jew who would not have withdrawn without stoning the woman.' So I said, 'You have your reply. You cannot see God who is a total stranger to you.'

Isn't there something similiar in the experience of each one of us? Isn't there in each one of us a resistance to God, a denial of God? When we seek him, do we not seek a God in our own image, a God who is convenient to us? Are we not prepared to reject the true God if we find him? Are we prepared to find God as he is, even if this encounter condemns us and upsets all the values which have hitherto been dear to us? Isn't the absence

of God in our life and in our prayers often due to the
fact that we are strangers to him and that if we did come
face to face with him we would not see him, or recognise
him? Isn't this what happened when Christ was on the
roads of Judea and Galilee? How many of his contem-
poraries met him, passed him by, without recognising or
even suspecting that there was something special about
him? Wasn't this the way he was seen by the crowds on
the road to Calvary? A criminal, a man who had caused a
breach of the peace – nothing else. Isn't this often the
way we think of God, even when we are able to feel
something of his presence? Don't we turn away from
him, because we sense that he will cause a breach of the
peace in our lives, upset its values? In this case we
cannot rely on encountering him in our prayer. I would
put it even more strongly, we should thank God with
all our hearts that he does not offer himself to us at this
moment, because we doubt him not like Job, but like
the bad thief on the cross. An encounter would be judgment and condemnation on us. We should learn to
understand this absence and judge ourselves because we
are not judged by God.

Another aspect of God's absence can be illustrated by
another story. A few years ago a young woman with an
incurable disease wrote to me. 'How grateful I am to God
for my illness. As my body weakens, I feel it becoming
more and more transparent to God's action.' I replied,
'Thank God for what he has given you, but do not expect
this state to last. The time will come when this natural
weakening will not continue to make you feel more
spiritual. Then you must rely on grace alone.' Some
months later she wrote to me again, 'I have become so
weak that I no longer have the strength to throw myself
on God. All I can do is to keep silent, surrender myself
hoping that God will come to me.' She added what is
the point of the story for us, 'Pray the Lord to give me

courage never to try and construct a false presence to fill the frightening void of his absence.'

I think these two stories need no comment. It is important that we rely on God. We must not rely on our own strength, neither must we rely on our own weakness. An encounter with God is a free act where God is in control and it is only when we are humble, as well as beginning to love God, that we are able to support his absence, to be enriched even by his absence.

BARTIMAEUS

Despairing hope is also one of the ways in which we can encounter God. We have several examples in the gospels and the lives of the saints. In the Gospel of St Mark, chapter 10 we have the story of Bartimaeus the blind beggar who sat at the gates of Jericho. The gospel story of his cure gives us certain crucial facts for the understanding of prayer. We are too often astonished that our prayer is not heard. We think we have only to offer a prayer for God to be obliged to answer it. In fact, if we strictly examine our motives for praying, and our needs, we see that we often do not pray for what is necessary to us but for what is superfluous. The ease with which we abandon our prayer when we are not heard proves that even when we are praying for something without which we ought not to be able to live, we have neither the patience nor the perseverance to insist on it. In the last resort we prefer to live without this necessity rather than fight desperately for it. A Father of the Church tells us that prayer is like an arrow. It is always capable of flying, of reaching its target, of piercing through resistance, but it only flies if it is shot from a good bow by a strong hand. It only hits the bull's eye if the archer's aim is steady and accurate. And what our prayer lacks is often this strength of spirit, the sense of the seriousness of our situation.

Bartimaeus is blind. We do not know if his eyes went slowly dim, the dear familiar world faded from his sight little by little, or whether he was born blind. But what we do see clearly is a grown man sitting by the dusty road begging. How many times in his life of perhaps thirty years must he have tried to regain his sight? How often must he have visited doctors, priests, healers, asked for prayers and help from whoever could give them? How often he must have hoped, with a hope that depends on men, reason and experience, but also on faith in mercy and compassion in the goodness and brotherhood of men? How often must this hope have sprung up only to wither unfulfilled? And now we find him by the roadside at the city gates, defeated by life, no longer seeking to recover his sight but trying merely to survive through the charity of the passers by. Not the burning charity which cherishes, but the cold charity which gives without compassion – money thrown anonymously to a hungry beggar, without even looking at him. The passerby is as blind as the beggar by the roadside, and his blindness is perhaps the greater because it is blindness of heart and conscience, he no longer has any part in human brotherhood. But this story takes place in the time of Christ. This blind beggar must have heard of this teacher who first appeared in Galilee and is now travelling throughout Judea and all the Holy Land, working miracles. A man who is said to cure the blind, to have given sight to a man born blind.

How this far off presence of a healing God must have revived his faith and hope but also his despair; hope because everything is possible to God, despair because nothing is possible to man. If God came to him, he could be cured. But how could he who was blind find this elusive miracle worker in Galilee or Judea, for he moved about continually and often appeared only to disappear almost at once? This way in which God's approach arouses both a last hope and an even deeper despair is true not only of Bartimaeus. It is also our own situation. God's presence like a sword separates the light from the darkness, but so often throws us back into the darkness because his presence dazzles us. It is because God is there, it is because eternal life is possible that it is so desperately urgent not to vegetate in a life which passes.

One day Bartimaeus sitting by the roadside hears a group of people go by. His practised ear discerns something particular about their walk, their conversation, their atmosphere. It is not a noisy crowd or caravan, this group has a centre. He asks the people passing, Who is it? They reply, Jesus of Nazareth. In a moment all the hope and despair of his life reach their climax. He is in deepest darkness and brightest light. He may be cured because God is walking by him. But he must seize the passing moment which will be gone in a twinkling. Jesus will only be within his reach for a few paces. Beforehand he will be too far away engrossed in conversation with others. Afterwards he will have passed beyond him for ever. Bartimaeus cries out his desperate hope. 'Jesus son of David have mercy on me.' This is in itself a profession of faith. The blind man must have thought it out in the months before when he heard all the stories of the cures worked by the Lord. For him, Jesus is not a wandering prophet. He is the son of David. Thus he calls him, begs him. And all around him voices are raised ordering to keep silence. How dare he interrupt the Master's conversation with his disciples? How dare he make such an unimportant request to the Master who is talking about the things of heaven? But he knows that his whole life, all the joy and despair of his life is in his blindness and the possibility of its cure. So he cries out and the more they try to silence him the louder he cries. And because he prays insistently for the one vitally important thing to him, he is heard, the Lord hears him, God cures him and opens a new life to him.

This is a very difficult lesson for us. How serious we must be about praying if we want our prayer to be worthy of the greatness of our destiny and of him who in all humility is willing to hear us. Despair, hunger for God, the vital necessity to us of what we ask, these are the conditions to make the arrow of our prayer fly sure to its target, aimed from a taut bow by a strong hand and a steady eye.

There is something special in this story which I should like to dwell on a little longer. It is the tumult surrounding this prayer as it reaches the Lord. For this encounter between the Lord and Bartimaeus took place in a double tumult. The inner tumult of his conflicting feelings of hope, despair, fear, excitement, and the tumult outside him, all the voices ordering him to silence because the Lord was busy with things worthier of his dignity and holiness. Bartimaeus is not the only one to encounter the Lord in tumult. Our whole life is an incessant tumult. It is a succession of situations demanding our presence, feelings, thoughts, heart and will in harmony, in contradiction and so on. And in this tumult our soul turns to the Lord, cries to him, and seeks rest in him. How often we think it would be so easy to pray if there was nothing to prevent us and how often this very tumult helps us to pray.

PRAYER IN TUMULT

But how can we pray in a state of turmoil? I should like to give a few examples to show how this is possible. I might almost call this turmoil an advantage, because like rugged rocks it helps us climb upwards when we cannot fly. The first story is taken from the *Lives of the Church Fathers*. An anonymous ascetic meets another ascetic, a man of prayer, in the mountains. They start a

conversation during which the visitor who is struck by
his companion's state of prayer, asks, 'Father who
taught you to pray without ceasing?' And his host, who
realises that his companion is a man of spiritual experience replies, 'I would not say this to everyone, but I will
tell you truly, that it was the demons.' The visitor says, 'I
think I understand you Father, but could you explain
in greater detail, how they taught you, so that I don't
misunderstand you.' And the other tells him the
following story: 'When I was young, I was illiterate and
I lived in a small village on the plain. One day I went
into church and heard the deacon reading the epistle of
St Paul which commands us to pray without ceasing.
When I heard these words, I was warmed with joy and
illuminated. At the end of the service I left the village
in great joy and retired to the mountains to live by
prayer alone. This state persisted in me for several hours.
Then night began to fall, it became colder and I began to
hear strange noises, footsteps and howls. Gleaming eyes
appeared. The wild beasts had come out of their lairs to
hunt the food that God had appointed them. I became
afraid, more and more afraid as the shadows deepened.
I spent the whole night in terror of the footsteps,
crackling sounds, shadows, gleaming eyes, the sense
of my own weakness knowing nowhere to turn for help.
Then I began to cry to God the only words that came to
my mind, words born of my fear, "Jesus, Son of David,
have mercy on me, sinner though I am." Thus the first
night passed. In the morning my fears vanished but I
began to be hungry. I looked for my food in bushes and
in the fields and it was hard to satisfy my hunger. And
as the sun was setting and I felt the terrors of the night
returning, I began to cry to God my fear and my hope.
Thus days passed and then months. I became accustomed
to the terrors of nature, but even as I prayed from moment to moment, new temptations and trials appeared.

The demons, the passions began to attack me on all sides, and just as the night beasts ceased to frighten me, the powers of darkness raged against my soul. I cried even more than before the same words to the Lord, "Lord, Jesus Christ, have mercy on me." This struggle went on for years. One day I reached the limits of my endurance. I had cried unceasingly to God in my agony and distress and I received no reply. God appeared to me implacable and then when the shred fibre of hope was breaking in my soul, I surrendered myself to the Lord saying, "You are silent, you don't care what becomes of me, but you are still my God and my Master and I will die here where I stand rather than abandon my quest." Suddenly the Lord appeared to me and peace came upon me and everything round me. The whole world had seemed to me in darkness and now I saw it bathed in divine light, shining with the grace of God's presence which sustains all that he has created. Then in a burst of love and gratitude, I cried to the Lord the only prayer that expressed all that was in me, "Lord Jesus Christ, have mercy on me, a sinner." And ever since, in joy, in suffering, in temptation and struggle or at the moment when peace comes to me, these words always spring from my heart. They are a song of joy, they are a cry to God, they are my prayer and my repentance.'

This example of the unknown ascetic shows how suffering, despair and turmoil bring these words out of us; this desperate cry, born of a hope that is stronger than despair itself, fed by despair and transcending it.

THE STILLING OF THE STORM

Often we are in tumult, perhaps less of a tumult than the young ascete, but we surrender to it and are defeated. That is why our prayer is trembling and hesitant, a prayer of tumult, uncertainty and incoherence. Isn't this the story of the storm on the lake of Galilee? The Lord and his disciples are on the lake. A tempest comes up when they are out to sea. Death threatens them, the waves are huge, the winds beat against them. They fight for their lives as hard as they can, and all this while the Lord is asleep on a cushion at the prow. He looks comfortable to them. They can't bear him looking so comfortable, his indifference. In their wretchedness they turn to him, wake him up, try to force him to realise what is happening. 'Lord, do you not see that we perish?' But what are they doing by asking this question? Are they appealing to the Lord to control the storm? Yes and no. First of all they want him to share their suffering. They want him to be as anxious as they are. They think he will not help them unless he shares their anxiety. The Lord gets up, he refuses to share their panic. He keeps his own serenity. First he turns to them, 'How long must I be with you, men of little faith?' And then he turns towards the storm, and casts his own serenity onto it. He orders the waves to be still and the wind to be silent, and his own peace to come down on everything about him. The storm is still and the disciples fall at his feet. Who is he? They are still doubtful. We often make the same mistake. Instead of seeking to share God's serenity, we ask God to share our tumult. Of course he does share it, but with his own serenity. This turmoil, disorder, disharmony, discord often enter our lives both in us and around us. They are caused by events we do not understand and human actions which are also tormented. And this is the essential problem, the link between the turmoil of life and our prayer, disturbance and serenity. We must realise in advance that in every confrontation between our inner peace and the hurly-burly of life, victory will go to the turmoil, because our prayer is weak and life is hard. Life is ruthless whereas our prayer, our inner peace and serenity is fragile. If we want to keep it and gain the victory over life, this must not be by open con-

frontation but as water waters the earth. The Fathers
said that water is an image of humility. It goes to the
bottom. This is quite true, but water is also invincible.
When through its weight it reaches the bottom, it begins
to rise and nothing can stop it. This is what our prayer
should do.

CONSTANT PRAYER

It is difficult to pray for a whole day. Sometimes we try
and imagine what it would be like. We think either of the
liturgical life of contemplative monks or else the
anchorite's life of prayer. We don't so often think of a
life of prayer taking place in ordinary life, when everything becomes prayer or an occasion for prayer. But this
is an easy way to pray, although it is of course very
demanding. Let us rise in the morning and offer ourselves to God. We have woken from a sleep which
divides us from yesterday. Waking up offers us a new
reality, a day which has never existed before, an unknown time and space stretching before us like a field
of untrodden snow. Let us ask the Lord to bless this day
and bless us in it. And when we have done this, let us
take our request seriously and also the silent answer we
have been given. We are blessed by God, his blessing will
be with us always in everything we do which is capable
of receiving this blessing. We will only lose it when we
turn away from God. And God will stay near us even
then, ready to come to our aid, ready to give us back the
grace we have rejected. We have put on the armour of
God, as St Paul says in Ephesians chapter 6. Faith, hope
and charity is our armour and also our cry to God. And
we begin this day in grace and glory, with the Lord's
cross and the Lord's death in us.

But the day itself is also blessed by God. Doesn't this
mean that everything that it contains, everything that
happens to us during it is within the will of God? Believ-

ing that things happen merely by chance is not believing in God. And if we receive everything that happens and everyone that comes to us in this spirit, we shall see that we are called to do the work of christians in everything. Every encounter is an encounter in God and in his sight. We are sent to everyone we meet on our way, either to give or to receive, sometimes without even knowing it. Sometimes we experience the wonder of giving what we did not possess, sometimes we have to pay with our own blood for what we give. We must also know how to receive. We must be able to encounter our neighbour in the way we tried to describe at the beginning of this essay. We must be able to look at him, hear him, keep silence, pay attention, be able to love and to respond wholeheartedly to what is offered, whether it be bitterness or joy, sad or wonderful. We should be completely open and like putty in God's hands. The things that happen in our life, accepted as God's gifts, will thus give us the opportunity to be continually creative, doing the work of a christian.

Too often christians have the habit whenever a problem or danger arises of turning to the Lord and crying, 'Lord protect us, save us, fight for us.' How often the Lord must look at us sadly and say to us in the silent language which we could understand if only our hearts were not so deafened by their fear, 'But I sent you into this situation to fight for me, are you not part of the army, the avant-garde of the kingdom which I have sent out to fight for me on earth? Did I not tell my apostles, "As my Father sent me, so I send you to live and die?" Have you forgotten the examples and counsels of the apostles?' It is for us to be Christ's presence on earth, sometimes victorious sometimes crucified. We must give ourselves always, and never run away. Everything is possible to us in the power of Christ, but it is for us to shed our blood, now it is for us to struggle and sweat. It is not for him

to come down and go through it all over again. Isn't this
the meaning of the conversation between Christ and
Peter whom he met at the gates of Rome trying to escape
from persecution, 'Where are you going Lord? Quo vadis
Domine?' 'I am going to Rome to be crucified again.'
Our job is to be present, not to be safe and sound. In
this day undertaken in God's name, we will have many
opportunities of asking what it means, what the successive things that happen mean. We must be able to
be quiet and meditative, look calmly at all the things that
puzzle us, for we will not be able to understand everything until we see God's whole plan. Our mistake is
nearly always supposing that human wisdom together
with plaintive prayer will be enough to solve the problems of eternal destiny. For everything, even the most
insignificant detail, is part of this eternal destiny, this
future of the world to which we belong. Human wisdom
must give way to the capacity to contemplate the mystery
before us, to try and discern the invisible hand of God,
whose wisdom is so different from human wisdom. But
his wisdom is also in the human heart. We must try and
be a silent balancing point in the tumult of life. We must
learn to wait till we understand. An English writer com-
pares the perfect christian to a sheepdog. A sheepdog,
says Evelyn Underhill, stops still when it hears its
master's voice, looks at its master and listens to its voice
to try and find out what he wants. The moment he understands he dashes off to do what its master wants. And,
Evelyn Underhill adds, the dog has a quality possessed
by very few christians – it never stops wagging its tail.

In our lives with all their turmoil and apparent disorder, we must try and discern God's plan by attentive
prayer and silent meditation. We should be able to find
courage, strength, inspiration and the advice we need in
our prayer. But this is an ideal situation; we cannot
venture into it immediately, because we are not yet ac-

customed to praying without cease, of being always
aware of ourselves and the life going on about us. We
must try to do this gradually, starting with a few hours
or less, because if we force ourselves too strenuously and
for too long to pay attention in this way, we will find it
beyond our strength and we will collapse. Not because
grace will fail us but because of our human weakness.
Then we will be disgusted and exhausted by prayer. The
most vital words will be like ashes in our mouths and we
will not feel we are living the day in and for God. In
these moments we must humbly accept defeat and realise that we are not yet strong enough to live constantly
in God's presence. Then we must fast spiritually, limit
our burst of prayer, particular prayer in words and know
that if we try and live through the day which we com-
mended to God in the morning, this is a prayerful situation in itself. Then gradually, as our will becomes
trained and the concentration of our heart and mind
improves, we will be able to spend whole days in prayer.
This prayer will not be merely the prayer of daily
life which cannot yet transform it, but a much more
conscious, deeper prayer, of which we will speak
again.

THE ROLE OF ASCESIS

What we have just said brings us to a problem which is
difficult for beginners to solve. This is the problem of
effortful prayer, ascesis. It is easy to pray in wonder or in
pain. It is much harder to pray on drab ordinary days,
when there is nothing within or without us to help us
pray. Then we must be able to force ourselves. Why?
Because our life of prayer should not only be our spontaneity, but also our firm unalterable conviction. This is
true of all our feelings, as well as our feelings about
praying. Are there not moments when we feel tired out
and if we were asked about our affection for those most

dear to us, we should have to say that we were incapable
of feeling it at the moment but that we were quite certain we had a very strong affection for them. But our
tiredness dominates our feelings. We can be spontaneous, but sometimes we are too tired and feel we
cannot feel. Then our affection resides in the will. But the
will together with firm conviction is the essential lever
in our life. If we force ourselves to do something purely
out of social convention, this constraint has a deadly
rather than a life-giving effect. Constraint need not be
sheer force, we can also add self-knowledge, knowledge
of others and kindness. When spontaneity and enthusiasm are lacking, we force ourselves to pray. Then we
must stand in God's presence by a pure act of faith; we
know that he exists and who he is. We approach him in
worship, in the reverent fear due to all that is holy. We
make a firm effort to pay the attention due to him. We
force ourselves to do this because we want to encounter
God not just for the immediate joy but for the longer-
lasting joy which will come to us when we have been
transformed by this contact with him and we live with
God's life. What we must do, without deceiving ourselves
or trying to deceive God, is to stand in his presence and
offer him even this unspontaneous prayer with firm
intellectual conviction and a determined will.

This means two things. First that we are not primarily
seeking the joy of an encounter with God but the deep
transformation that God alone can work in us, that we
are prepared, as the Church Fathers said, to give our
blood in order to receive the Spirit. And secondly it
means that our prayer must be the most accurate possible
expression of our true convictions. When we pray in
our own words our prayer should be sober, attentive and
humble. It should express the reality of its own poverty
as well as our firm convictions and desire. This requires
a strong effort of detachment. But such detachment is

one of the elements necessary to any encounter. If we
use 'ready made' prayers (prayers made by others in
suffering or in spontaneous enthusiasm) we must be careful not to lie to God under the pretext of offering prayers
worthy of him.

THE CONSOLATION OF THE SCRIPTURES

For periods of dryness we also need some prayers in
reserve, which have meant a lot to us at other times.
These prayers which have expressed our minds and
hearts can be offered to God when we feel we have little
to express. But sometimes we need to qualify them.
There are prayers suitable to luminous moments in our
lives which cannot be simply repeated as an act of faith
in ourselves. When we are full of doubt, we cannot say
to the Lord, 'Lord my heart is ready, my heart is ready.'
And there are many other prayers the same. We must
alter them a bit, so that we tell God the truth. We must
find a balance between expressing our firm conviction
and distorting our present reality. It is important to be
able to use these prayers to wake ourselves up or bring
ourselves back to life. For life comes from the Word of
God. In dreary times we can recommend two things. We
can start from a scripture text. When we feel low and
sad, we can still sow the word, and perhaps we are more
capable than we think of receiving it and bearing fruit.
We should choose scriptural texts which we usually find
moving, texts we have often thought about and responded
to, which mean something in our lives and have per-
meated it like the leaven the woman added to the dough.
We should re-read them when we feel unenthusiastic.
And from them we can offer a prayer which may seem
cold and dead to us, but which is at least truthful. We
should not of course only pray from the scriptures in
moments when we have to force ourselves to pray. It is
always a good way of praying. But we need it paricu-

larly in bad moments, because the word of God is powerfully creative, it reaches beyond the depths of our souls,
it is life and can give us life, because it is God himself
speaking.

BEARING WITH OURSELVES

If we use prayers made by the saints (as I have said they
are useful to have in reserve) when we cannot think up
our own, it is difficult in these times when we feel dead
to know who to pray to. God seems to be absent, the
heavens are empty and we feel as if we are crying out in
despair with no one to hear us. Do you know these
passages from Emile Verhaeren:

> Worshipfully
> the winter night offers its pure cup to heaven.
> And I raise my heart, my benighted heart.
> Lord my heart, to your emptiness.
> But I know you will not answer.
> You do not exist, my heart's desire.
> I know you are a lie and my lips pray
> and my knees. Your large hands are shut,
> your large eyes withdrawn from my despair.
> I know you are my imagination.
> Lord have pity on my hopelessness.
> To your silence I must cry.
> The winter night offers its pure cup to heaven.
>
> Darkness.
> I am here, the other is elsewhere, the silence doesn't
>   give
> We are unhappy. Satan passes us through his sieve.
>
> We both suffer and there is no road
> between us, neither hand nor word.
>
> Only the common night incommunicable
> when we cannot work and love is not possible.

I listen, I am alone and it frightens me.
I hear the sound of her voice, I hear a cry.

I feel a slight wind ruffle my hair.
From the jaws of the beast, from death, save her.

Again I feel death between my teeth.
My stomach turns, I catch my breath.

Alone in the winepress I trod grapes deliriously
all night from wall to wall, laughing wildly.

Will he who made our eyes not see me?
And he who made our ears not hear me?

I know that where sin is great, your mercy is greater
   still.
In the hour of the Prince of this world, deliver us
   from evil.

When God seems absent, the heavens empty and the
void immense, we should direct our prayer not to him
but talk to ourselves. We should address each word of
our prayer to our own depressed and dormant soul. We
must treat our soul like a mother taking a naughty child
onto her lap and telling him a story. At first the child
ignores her then he begins to pay attention. In the same
way we should begin by saying each word only for its
bare meaning, without reflecting on its weight. First we
say the words and simply understand them with our
mind, then we offer them to our heart, repeat a phrase
or part of a phrase perhaps once, twice, three times, to
try and kindle what is still alive in us, under the ashes.
We must not straitjacket our will, but let it lie comfort-
ably at rest. For rest is part of ascesis. We should be
able to let ourselves go, be supple, not passive but in an
attitude of surrender. We should listen intelligently and
respond with all that is still alive in us to the familiar
words, to words spoken in deserts, by heroes in prayer

and the life in God. If we simply listen to these words, without effort, without adding to our weariness and exhaustion, then repeat them, try to savour them and feel their weight, often after a while, perhaps a long while, these words restore us to life, first our heart, then our will, and make us active again, capable of the sublime action of prayer.

In this situation our body, which is so often a nuisance to us in our life of prayer, can be immensely valuable. This body which is a member of the body of Christ and fed by the sacraments, can restore our soul. For the body plays an active part in our inner life. It has a part, felt or unfelt, in every movement of the soul, every feeling, thought, act of will or transcendent experience. The body's response is two-fold. It plays its part in our effort of concentration and it adapts to the object of that concentration. This does not happen just anyhow. Different parts of the body are involved in different objects of concentration, and thinking or feeling about the same object, with greater or lesser purity, in a more active or more passive way, also involves different parts of the body. Only daydreams cannot fix themselves, they wander at will like, according to Theophanos the Recluse 'a disorderly swarm of flies' or, according to Ramakrishna 'monkeys jumping from branch to branch'. As soon as a commanding thought or feeling engages us, all our physical activity groups round it, acquires a greater simplicity and cohesion. The field of consciousness narrows and defines a physical space of attention with its accompanying somato-psychic characteristics.

The ascesis of constraint, corporal ascesis is the only way of establishing prayer in complete stability. Spontaneous prayer, born of wonder or suffering is too dependent on incident. Only prayer born of conviction and a steady will can establish us face to face with God. The supreme prayer of stability in the orthodox church, called the prayer of Jesus is: 'Lord Jesus Christ, son of God, have mercy on me'.

GOD'S SILENCE AND MAN'S SILENCE

This encounter between God and us in stable prayer always leads to silence. We have to learn to distinguish two sorts of silence. God's silence and our own inner silence. First the silence of God, often harder to bear than his refusal, the absent silence we spoke of earlier. Second, the silence of man, deeper than speech, in closer communion with God than any words. God's silence to our prayer can last only a short time or it may seem to go on for ever. Christ was silent to the prayers of the Canaanite woman and this led her to gather up all her faith and hope and human love to offer to God so that he might extend the conditions of his kingdom beyond the chosen people. The silence of Christ provoked her to respond, to grow to her capacity. And God may do the same to us with shorter or longer silences to summon our strength and faithfulness and lead us to a deeper relationship with him than would have been possible had it been easy. But sometimes the silence seems frighteningly final to us. Do you know the words of Alfred de Vigny:

If, as we read, the Son of man
cried in the sacred Garden
and was not heard,
if heaven abandons us for dead,
we should spurn God's unjust absence
and render silence for silence.

Isn't this the impression that many christians are left with after reading the account of the agony in the Garden? And this silence is a problem for us which we have to solve, the problem of prayer which apparently receives no answer at all. If we read the gospel we find that the only prayer to God which is not heard is the prayer of Christ in Gethsemane. We should remember this because all too often we try and interpret God's silence as man's or God's insufficiency. When we are trying to defend God's honour we say my faith or your faith was not great enough for God to reply with a miracle. When our faith is weak we say, perhaps God could not reply, through impotence or indifference. But we have nothing to say to Christ's own prayer remaining unanswered. The faith of Christ the Son of God must be perfect. We cannot doubt God's love for him and does not Christ himself say that his Father could send twelve legions of angels to deliver him? If Christ is abandoned, that is because God has foreseen something better will come of it for us, at the price of his life. In this and other prayers in the gospel we see that a prayer remains fruitless if it is not supported by faith. Do you remember the passage where Christ was unable to work any miracles in Nazareth because of their unbelief? As soon as there is faith, then the conditions are present for a miracle, that is the kingdom of God come in power. And without intrusion, simply because he is the Lord of his kingdom, Christ acts with sovereign power, answers our prayers, helps us and saves us. But when our faith is firmly anchored in him we become capable of sharing his care for the world; we share in his solitude in the face of God's silence. We should realise that God's silence is either an appeal to forces dormant in us, or else has already taken their measure, and offers us a share in Christ's redemptive work.

God's silence and absence, but also man's silence and absence. An encounter does not become deep and full until the two parties to it are capable of being silent with one another. As long as we need words and actions, tangible proof, this means we have not reached the depth and fulness we seek. We have not experienced the silence which enfolds two people in common intimacy. It goes deep down, deeper than we knew we were, an inner silence where we encounter God, and with God and in God our neighbour.

In this state of silence we do not need words to feel close to our companion, to communicate with him in our deepest being, beyond ourselves to something which unites us. And when the silence is deep enough, we can begin to speak from its depths, but carefully and cautiously so as not to break it by the noisy disorder of our words. Then our thought is contemplative. Our mind instead of trying to make distinctions between many forms, as it usually does, tries to elicit simple luminous forms from the depths of the heart. The mind does its true work. It serves him who expresses something greater than it. We look into depths beyond ourselves and try to express something of what we find with awe and reverence. Such words, if they do not try to trivialise or intellectualise the total experience, do not break the silence, but express it. There is a remarkable passage by a medieval carthusian writer which says that if Christ is the Word of God, the Father is the creative silence which can only produce a word adequate to itself, a perfect expression of it.

We feel something of this in our moments of silence. Sometimes this silence comes upon us like a miracle, like a gift of God. More often we have to learn to make room for it in ourselves. We must have faith, endurance and hope and also that inner peace which the Greek fathers call *hesychia*. Contemplation requires this silence, which cannot be defined as either activity or passivity. It is a serene watchfulness. But we must also learn through bodily and spiritual ascesis to attain this perfect prayer of inner silence. I will not dwell on this point here. There is more about it in the books listed at the end of this essay.

THE SEARCH FOR SILENCE

We seek for silence in both a human and a divine way. We must both seek it ourselves and hope for it as a gift. The human search is described for us in a remarkable manner in the medieval writings of Fr. Laurence on the Practice of the Presence of God. In a much humbler fashion I should like to tell the story of an old woman who had prayed for many years without ever perceiving the presence of God but who finally found it in silence. Shortly after my ordination to the priesthood I was sent into an old people's home to celebrate Christmas with them. A very old woman came to me. She told me that she had constantly recited the prayer of Jesus for many years but she had never been given the experience of the presence of God. Young as I was, I found a simple answer to her problem, 'How can God get a word in edgeways if you never stop talking. Give him a chance. Keep quiet'. 'How can I do that?' she said. I then gave her some advice which I have since given to others because it worked on that occasion. I advised her after breakfast to tidy her room and make it as pleasant as possible and sit down in a position where she could see the whole room, the window onto the garden, the icons with their little oil lamps. 'When you have sat down, rest for a quarter of an hour in the presence of God, but take care not to pray. Be as quiet as you can and as you obviously can't do nothing, knit before the Lord and tell me what happens.' After a few days she came back happily. She had felt the presence of God. I asked her curiously what had happened. She said she had done exactly what I had suggested. She sat down and looked about her quietly and peacefully feeling she had the right to be inactive and not praying and for the first time for years, she said, she noticed that the room was peaceful and pleasant to be in. She looked at it and saw

it for the first time. There was an encounter between her
and the place she had lived in for many years without
ever seeing. Then she became aware of the peace and
silence round her, a peace and silence accentuated by the
ticking of her clock and the clicking of her needles on the
arms of her chair. Gradually this silence which had been
outside her came within her and enveloped her. The
silence took her out of herself into a richer silence which
was not just the absence of noise but rich in itself and
at its centre she found a presence. And when she felt
this presence she was moved to pray but from the depths
of this silence, not in floods of words and a whirl of
thoughts, but gently and quietly taking each word from
the silence and offering it to God. Of its own accord her
prayer had become the expression of her inner silence
and part of the silence of God which she had felt. This
is a method easy for everyone to try. It means of course
contending with the whirl of thoughts, the heart's hesi-
tations, the body's restlessness and the giddiness of the
will. There are many exercises based on ascesis and
psychology But even without these, simply letting go of
ourselves before God into the depth of silence we are
capable of, will help us make great progress.

Sometimes this silence comes to us from God even
more plainly. Without any warning we suddenly find
ourselves silently at rest in God. Praying for others is
shedding our blood, spending ourselves to the limit in
sympathy and compassion. But praying for others is also
going the way of Christ, becoming an expression of his
intercession, uniting ourselves with him in his prayer
and his incarnation. We experience the unutterable
groans of the Spirit in our own hearts. And the greater
our sympathy and the more closely we identify through
compassion with those for whom we pray, the more perfect is our communion with the merciful God. Our prayer
rising out of human suffering leads us to the heart of

God's mystery. First we are achingly aware of earthly suffering, then as our prayer continues we become more aware of the presence of God and a moment comes when we lose sight of the earth and are carried away into the depths of God. Rest, silence, peace and then at the heart of the mystery of love we find again those for whom we felt such compassion. The Spirit of love, the Spirit of God comes into us and leads us back to earth. But now our earthly involvement is bound together with the contemplation of the living God, the God of love.

This silence leads us to an encounter with God in serene and simple faith, to what is sometimes called the 'prayer of simple regard', expressed so beautifully by the peasant of Ars who when asked by his saintly priest what he did when he sat hour after hour in church without even fingering his rosary, 'I look at him and he looks at me and we are happy together'. But this prayer of simple regard is not just prayer it is also a transforming power. In a remarkable book which I have already mentioned, *La Réponse du Seigneur* by Alphonse de Chateaubriand, we find the following passage describing how the contemplative prayer of simple regard transformed a child who prayed thus of his own accord, not only inside but also outside.

'It was in a small remote mountain village nestling under a huge granite rock which had, by an accident of nature, a large human figure carved on it. This face dominated the country round it both because it was so big and because of its majestic expression. Beneath it the village looked like a small kite or merlin's nest. The people of the village believed that one day a very good man who looked exactly like the figure on the mountainside would come to their hamlet to practice his virtue and to do great good.

This is what they said during the long evenings, to

instruct their children, to reawaken happy memories in the old, to give hope to the sick. There was one little boy who had also heard the story and retained such a deep impression of it that he never stopped thinking about it and looking at the figure on the rock. He often sat on his doorstep with his finger in the corner of his mouth and looked up to the huge giant towering over the people below. He would stop in the middle of his games and think about the wonderful promise. What treasures would the hero bring? He became more and more attached to the carved figure and gradually grew to look like him.

This lasted throughout his childhood ... Until one day he was walking through the village square and his friends and neighbours looked at him with amazement and saw that he of whom the ancient tradition spoke was among them.'

The example of the monk Sylvanus shows us that prayer gives us both God and man, man and God. As we said at the beginning, this vision of things in depth gives us knowledge of all reality, our visible neighbours and our invisible Neighbour.

PRAYER AND OUR NEIGHBOUR

This leads us to our final point in our consideration of this encounter, encounter with the human community. This human community comes to us in two very different ways. On the one hand it is a secular community, the total human world about us, which we are part of. On the other hand it is the community of the church which we are also part of. In the secular community the christian has to be the presence of Christ. This means a total commitment. The central action of the economy of salvation is the incarnation of the word of God, an act by which the free transcendent God becomes one of

us, involved with us, forever. The christian must be involved in the same way. Did not Christ say, 'As my
Father sent me, so I send you'. Did he not add that he
was sending us out as sheep among wolves. Did he not
say that we must be in the world but not of the world?
This gives us the obligation to meet the world as a whole,
each member of the human community personally, but
in a new way, in God's sight and in God. And also to
judge everything in a new way, in God's way, who did
not come to judge the world but to save it, God who so
loved the world that he gave his only son for its salvation. In the gospel there is a radical change of values in
the encounter between God and man. Not that good
and evil lose their meaning, but evil is seen as a wound,
as a sickness troubling our neighbour and from which we
also suffer. We can hate evil and love our neighbour very
much, to the death. A Russian martyr bishop said that it
is a privilege for a christian to die as a martyr because
only a martyr can stand before God on the day of judgment and defend his persecutors. 'Lord in your name
and following your example, I forgive them. Ask nothing
further of them.' And this upsetting of values is ruled
by the mystery of the cross, the innocent dying for the
guilty. We see three crosses on Calvary. Two thieves and
the Son of God made man. The thief on Jesus's left
judges by human values – if human justice has committed
the crime of crucifying the innocent, it loses the right to
be called justice. The criminal can appeal against it, curse
it, reject it, deny it. He dies in a state of rebellion. The
thief on Jesus's right sees that human justice can act
unjustly and condemn the innocent, but also the guilty.
He accepts his own suffering and condemnation because
an innocent man is suffering with him. He finds peace
and goes to paradise. Since the passion of our Lord Jesus
Christ, since God made man appeared as a criminal, we
can no longer judge the criminal in the same way as the

ancient world, we can no longer trust completely the evidence of our reason and our senses.

In God's sight we see the actions we condemn and should be ready to give our lives for the person who did the wrong. When we are the victims of these actions, we receive an extra power, the divine power of forgiving these wrongs now and for eternity. This means that our prayer is a situation in which we present to God all the things that happen in a world that is estranged from him. Our prayer has a priestly function. We should sacrifice our own ego. We are a royal priesthood called to make all things holy. We condemn the evil we see done, but the doer is our brother and we must pray and live and die for him. This is the meaning of intercession which we discuss later on.

We discover God in Christ in the community of the church. True christian encounter includes the visible world with both its outward and inward face, and the God of this world with all his invisible reality. Christian encounter should include the whole universe. The unbeliever does not see the invisible world. Unfortunately the christian is sometimes also blind to the visible world and thinks this a virtue. The whole human community with all its problems, all its future both temporal and eternal should be of interest to the christian. Christian prayer should be wide enough to contain it all. If we remembered more often that everything is important, nothing is profane except when we make it so by denying its holiness, we would have fewer distractions in our prayers. The world can distract us from God in our prayers. But when we are worried about something and unable to encounter God in silence, we often try mistakenly to put our worry out of our mind, as if it were a barrier between us and God. We think it wrong that anything else could claim our attention when we are in the presence of God. I think that often we could encounter God by sharing our worry with him instead of trying to push it aside. We ought to present it to God in detail but with precision and sobriety. We should present it as a mother brings a child to a doctor she trusts. We should say to God, 'This is all I can talk about to you at the moment. You who know everything look at my problem, understand it with your own understanding.'

When we have thus offered a person or a situation to God, we should be able to become detached from it. This requires faith and the ease with which we can detach ourselves from a care, is the measure of our faith. If we can say, 'Lord now I have told you everything, my heart is peaceful and I can rest in you.' If our heart is really at peace, if our mind is really freed from worrying, then our faith is complete. We have laid our burden at God's feet and now he is carrying it on his broad shoulders. Let us be encouraged by the story of the monk who was praying for his neighbours and who gradually lost consciousness of the earth because he became so wrapped up in God and who then found all his neighbours again in God. It should show us how easy it is to encounter God when we are troubled, if we offer him our troubles in true charity, not in selfishness. For he is the God of history, he created us, he became man in the fullest and most painful, richest and poorest sense of the word to save us and bring us to him. By our prayer of compassion we should be as involved in the human situation, as Christ was by his incarnation. We should engage in action which supports our prayer and makes it truthful. Prayer without action is a lie. This is the fundamental nature of intercession.

INTERCESSION

Interceding does not mean reminding God of things he has forgotten to do. It is placing ourselves at the heart of a troubled situation. Here is an example from the time of the Great War and the civil war in Russia, when the country was engaged in war abroad and at home. In a small provincial village which had just changed hands, a young woman of twenty-seven or so was trapped with her two small children. Her husband belonged to the opposite side. She had been unable to escape in time and she was in hiding, trying to save her own and her children's lives. She spent a day and a night in great fear and the following evening the door of her hiding place opened and a young woman, a neighbour of her own age, came in. She was a simple woman with nothing extraordinary about her. She said, 'Is So and So your name?' The mother replied 'Yes' in great fear. The neighbour said, 'You have been discovered, they are coming for you tonight to shoot you. You must leave.' The mother looked at her children and said, 'Where shall I go? How can I get away with these children. They could not walk fast enough or far enough for us not to be caught.' And this neighbour suddenly became a neighbour in the full sense of the gospel. She approached the mother and said with a smile, 'They will not go after you, because I will stay here in your place.' The mother must have said, 'They will shoot you.' She replied, 'Yes but I have no children. You *must* leave.' And the mother went. I do not tell this simply as a story of sacrifice. I should like to dwell on certain points which gives it a particular significance in Christ and, through the cross, lead us to the idea of the resurrection and the life of him who is greater than us in those who are smaller.

NATHALIE IN CHRIST

The mother went out and the young woman stayed behind. Her name was Nathalie. I do not want to try and imagine what happened that night. I should simply like to point out a few parallels. Night fell, an autumn

night, which became colder and wetter and darker. This
young woman, alone, expecting nothing from anyone
except death, faced this death she was about to suffer
for no reason – she was young and healthy and they were
not after her. Remember the Garden of Olives. In the
darkening there was a man, also young, in his thirties,
whose friends were all asleep, waiting for death, waiting
for them to come for him, because he had accepted
death in our place. And we know the story in the gospel,
his anguish, his cry to his Father, his sweat of blood. We
know that when he could no longer bear his loneliness
he went to see if his disciples were awake and then went
back to face his death alone, a death for others, impossible, absurd. This is the first image, Nathalie in
Christ.

Nathalie must have gone to the door more than once
and thought to herself. 'I have only to push it open and
I am no longer N.. I'll be Nathalie again and not con-
demned to death.' But she did not go out. We can
imagine what her terror must have been like when we
remember the courtyard of the house of Caiphas. Peter
the rock, the strong one who had said to Christ that if
the whole world denied him, he would not deny him,
that he would die for him. Peter met a servant girl who
had only to say, 'You also were with him' for Peter to
answer 'I do not know the man', for Peter to deny Christ
twice more and for Christ to turn and look at him.
Nathalie could have surrendered too and said, 'I shall
not die, I'll escape.' But she did not. This young woman of
about thirty resisted in Christ, when Peter failed him.

And this young woman must also have wondered
whether her death might not be in vain. All very well to
die to save a woman and her children, but what if the
woman were caught and also killed. Remember the
man who was the greatest among those born of woman
– John the Baptist. At the end of his life, when his death

was also near, St John the Baptist sent two of his
disciples to ask Christ, 'Are you the one who is to come
or must we wait for another?' What a weight of suffering
there is in this question which sounds so simple. He was
about to die for being the fore-runner, the prophet and
baptiser of Christ and just before his death, doubt
entered. 'What if I made a mistake, what if he whom I
prophesied is still to come, and he to whom I bore witness is the wrong man?' Then his hard life in the desert
would have been in vain. He was called a voice crying in
the wilderness, not a prophet speaking in God's name,
but the voice of God speaking through him because he
was totally identified with that voice. And now he was
near death if Jesus of Nazareth is really the one, then it
was all worth it, but if he is not, then God himself has
deceived him. And like Nathalie in her hiding place,
the prophet received no answer, or rather he received
a prophet's answer: 'Go and tell John what you have
seen, the blind see, the lame walk and the poor have the
gospel preached to them. Blessed is he who is not
offended by me.' In his prison he had to confront his
past, his present and his death, alone. And Nathalie also
received no reply. I could have told her now that N.. was
saved, that her children are now more than fifty years
old. I could have told her other things too, but she
never knew. She was shot in the night.

But there is something else to intercession besides
sacrifice. As well as the cross and Gethsemane there is
also the resurrection, a resurrection conformed to our
share in the mystery of Christ but also to our human
littleness. You remember the passage in St Paul where
he says, 'I live, not I, Christ lives in me.' Sometimes we
might wonder what these words mean exactly. N.. and
her children know one thing, theirs are henceforth borrowed lives. Their own lives died with Nathalie, she goes
on living through them. They live because she died. She

took their death on her, gave them her life. They live with a life that belongs to her.

THE INTERCESSION OF CHRIST

This human story illustrates something very important about salvation. It shows us the hard reality of intercession. We often intercede. We pray to God to be merciful and kind to those in need. But intercession is more than this. The word in Latin means to take a step which puts us at the heart of a situation, like a man who stands between two people about to fight. The first image that comes to mind is from Job chapter nine, where this man who has suffered so greatly says 'Where is there a man who will stand between me and my judge?' Where is the man with the courage to stand between God and his poor creature, in order to separate and unite them. To separate them from the opposition which makes each a prisoner of the other and to unite them in the freedom of harmony restored. And this man is Christ, Christ who is God the Word Incarnate, he takes the step, to stand between fallen man and God. He is God's equal and man's equal, one with God because he is God, one with man because he is man and prepared to take the consequences of his divine love upon his human flesh. This is intercession, this is what it means to take that step into the heart of a situation for ever, for all eternity, because Christ born of the Virgin is both he who died on the cross and he who rose from the dead and carried his human flesh to the heart of the mystery of the Trinity in his Ascension.

We see through the example of Nathalie that Christ is really the Way, the way to live, the very being of the christian, the sole human and divine reality. He is the way to life, life so full and overflowing that it gives eternity both to him who lives it and those near him, at the price of the cross. It is the martyr's victory, the

victory of the weak over the strong, the victory of the
vulnerable, human and divine love over what appears
invincible, hatred which exhausts itself and has only
one time.

THE IMAGE OF THE MOTHER OF JESUS

Besides Nathalie's heroic sacrifice, we are committed to
the world in another way, simply by our presence. 'You
are in the world but not of the world,' Christ said. I think
the best illustration is the story of Mary the mother of
Jesus at Cana of Galilee. Some humble people are cele-
brating a wedding. They are good and upright people who
have invited Christ to their wedding and he has not
refused to come. His mother is also there and his disciples. The moment comes in the midst of the feast
when the wine runs out. There follows a disjointed
sounding conversation. Mary says, 'They have no more
wine'. 'Woman, what is there between you and me?'
Christ answers, 'my hour has not yet come'. Instead of
telling her son that she is his mother and the hour for
kindness and compassion is always come, Mary says
nothing. She simply turns to the servants and says,
'Whatever he tells you, do it'. And Christ contrary to
what he has just said, blesses the washing water and it
becomes the wine of the kingdom. How can we understand this conversation and the contradiction between
Christ's words and actions? Doesn't Christ's question to
his mother mean something like this? 'What relationship gives you the right to approach me thus? Is it because you are my natural mother who gave me birth, is
it because you are my closest natural relation? If this is
why, I can do nothing, because the kingdom has not yet
come.' And Mary instead of answering him, brings the
kingdom by showing that she has perfect faith in him,
that the words she has pondered in her heart from the
beginning have been fruitful and she sees him for what

he is, the word of God. But then conditions are right for
the kingdom. God is present because she has given herself to him completely, with total faith. He can act
freely, without forcing nature, because he is in his own
domain. So he works the first miracle of the gospel.

We too can be in the same situation as Mary. We too
can make God's kingdom come, wherever we are, in spite
of the unbelief of the people we are with. Simply by
having complete faith in the Lord and thus showing ourselves to be children of the kingdom. This is a crucially
important act of intercession. The fact that we are present in a situation alters it profoundly because God is then
present with us through our faith. Wherever we are, at
home with our family, with friends when a quarrel is
about to begin, at work or even simply in the under-
ground, the street, the train, we can recollect ourselves
and say, 'Lord I believe in you, come and be among us'.
And by this act of faith, in a contemplative prayer which
does not ask to see, we can intercede with God who has
promised his presence when we ask for it. Sometimes we
have no words, sometimes we do not know how to act
wisely, but we can always ask God to come and be
present. And we shall see how often the atmosphere
changes, quarrels stop, peace comes. This is not a minor
mode of intercession, although it is less spectacular than
a great sacrifice. We see in it again how contemplation
and action are inseparable, that christian action is impossible without contemplation. We see also how such
contemplation is not a vision of God alone, but a deep
vision of everything enabling us to see its eternal meaning. Contemplation is a vision not of God alone, but of
the world in God.

THE CHURCH IS A MYSTERY OF ENCOUNTER

Within the total human community, there is a community which alone is capable of grasping our

transcendent vocation. This is the church, a chosen community, whose members are not chosen for privilege but for duty. Christ told us he was sending us out as sheep among wolves. He ordered us to go. On the eve of his resurrection he told us that as his Father had sent him, he sent us. He told us we were like a heavenly colony on earth, an avant-garde of the kingdom of God, fellow soldiers with the Lord in the battle to free the world from the powers of evil and death. The Church can only be defined from the outside. Within it is the mystery of being in God, the mystery of encounter, presence and communion. It is not a human community turned towards God, obedient to God, centred on God. It is a living body and this body is both human and divine. It has a visible aspect, us, and an invisible, God, and us in God and God in us. In one respect the church, as St Ephraem the Syrian defines it is not the assembly of the just, but of sinners on the way to repentance. It cries to God in its suffering and needs his salvation. In its other aspect, it is not simply on the way, it has arrived. God is with it and it has his peace. Its nature is complex and is revealed both in the sinner needing salvation and in the incarnate word, true God and true man. He gives the full measure of humanity which is the temple of the Holy Spirit. The Holy Spirit makes us members of Christ's body, the whole Christ we shall one day become, in the daring phrase of one Father of the Church 'only son in the only son'. The Holy Spirit is the Spirit of God who teaches us to call the Father of the word, our Father.

The church is a mysterious body in which we become through the Spirit what Christ is, just as he became what we are. In the church our lives are hidden with Christ in God. The dimension of the church which makes it essentially different from the world is the eschatological dimension. It already belongs to the age to come.

That is why the Spirit of God is present in the church's life. That is why we address him in the eucharistic prayers. The kingdom is already present, in which all will be fulfilled. God is already all in all, just as he is already in the bread and wine. And it is because the church knows things not only in their present sadness but in their final fulfilment, that it can give thanks from this sad and often bestial world for all things. She gives thanks for their ultimate fulfilment, not for their present state which would be unforgivable by the world and by God. We should be able to turn to the Lord from our own experience and say, 'Lord you are just in all your doings, you are right'. And the Church can only do this because of her vision of the end. She sees not only the world darkened by sin but the world transfigured, in which the resurrection and eternal life are already present.

And that is why the church makes no distinction between the living and the dead. God is not the God of the dead, he is the God of the living. For him all men are alive, and so they are for the church. Within this eschatological perspective we can see death as the great hope and joyfully await the judgment and the coming of Christ. We can say with the Spirit of the church 'Come soon, Lord Jesus'. History and eternity are one eschatologically and eucharistically. The prayer of the church includes not only the members of the church but through them and because of them, the whole world. She sees the whole world as the potential church, the total church for which she hopes. And in the church, within this eschatology, all things are already accomplished as well as being in process. We have a living relationship in the communion of saints and sinners with all the living and the dead.

THE LIVING AND THE DEAD

What does it mean to pray for the dead? Are we asking the Lord to act unjustly? Certainly not. By our prayer, we bear witness that the dead have not lived in vain. We show that as well as the many worthless things they did in their lives, they also sowed the seed of charity. We pray for them with love and gratitude, we remember their presence among us. And our prayer for them must be supported by our lives. If we do not bear fruit in our lives of what the dead have taught us, our prayer for them will be feeble indeed. We must be able to say, 'Look Lord, this man lived and made me love him, he gave me examples to follow and I follow them'. The day will come when we shall be able to say, 'The good that you see in my life is not mine; he gave me it, take it and let it be this for his glory, perhaps for his forgiveness'. Do you know the prayer that was reported in the *Sud Deutsche Zeitung* of the man who died in a concentration camp:

'Peace to all men of evil will. Let vengeance cease and punishment and retribution. The crimes have gone beyond measure, our minds can no longer take them in. There are too many martyrs ... Lord do not weigh their sufferings on your scales of justice, and let them not be written in their act of accusation and demand redress. Pay them otherwise. Credit the torturers, the informers and traitors with their courage and strength of spirit, their dignity and endurance, their smile, their love, their broken hearts which did not give in even in the face of death, even in times of greatest weakness ... take all this into account Lord for the remission of the sins of their enemies, as the price of the triumph of justice. Take good and not evil into account. And let us remain in our enemies' thoughts not as their victims, not as a nightmare, but as those who helped them overcome their crimes. This is all we ask for them.'

The life of each one of us does not end at death on this earth and birth into heaven. We place a seal on everyone we meet. This responsibility continues after death, and the living are related to the dead for whom they pray. In the dead we no longer belong completely to this world, in us the dead still belong to history. Prayer for the dead is vital, it expresses the totality of our common life.

THE SAINTS

We also pray not only for certain people but to certain people. We pray to Mary and the saints. But we do not pray to them to turn away God's strict justice by their gentleness. We know that their will and God's are one and this harmony includes in charity all the living and the dead. If it is true that our God is not the God of the dead but of the living, isn't it natural that we should pray to those who are particularly shining examples for us. We can each find among the saints one that particularly attracts us. We do not make a radical distinction between those who are saints and those who are not. Certain saints were set apart by God as examples for all christians. This does not mean that others were not. And it is quite proper for us to pray to our dead parents and friends without this being blasphemy.

Our prayers to Mary are particularly important. She is closest to Christ of any human being. Not because she gave birth to him, but because she was truly his mother not only physically but also spiritually. When we pray to her we should remember that our sins caused the death of Christ on the cross and she is his mother. We can pray to her as follows: 'Mother, I killed your son,

if you forgive me, no one will dare condemn me'. This
expresses our faith in her charity.

LITURGICAL PRAYER

We must now say a few words about liturgical prayer.
This prayer which is always going on in the church, may
seem to lack spontaneity. It is indeed rigidly structured,
because its aim is not only to express collective human
spontaneity, but also to educate it. It is also an expression of beauty, but not just of the beauty which is
present but of what the world could be, what God wishes
it to be. We could discuss many details of the liturgy of
the orthodox church, the actions, the icons, the bible
readings. The liturgy is a school for spirituality, it is a
situation and an encounter with God and the world in
God. It has its own spontaneity which goes beyond the
actual spontaneity of each of its members. It is the holy
spontaneity of the community already fulfilled and in
God. In the sacraments we come face to face with God
not only through the word and its invisible grace but
also through visible things. The waters of baptism become
the primordial waters of life and also the water promised
by Christ to the Samaritan woman. In the bread and
wine which have already become the body and blood of
Christ, we prefigure the day when God will be all in
all. In the church we encounter God and the world in
God. The christian must also meet the world, in all its
sadness and serve it like the son of God made man. He
must be totally involved in this incarnation, it is part of
being human and in it his prayer becomes intercession
and intercession becomes the sacrifice of Calvary.

There is a tension between ecstatic encounter with God
and our presence in the world. It is impossible to live
God's life to the full without losing contact with earthly
life. 'This,' says Symeon the new theologian, 'happens
not to the perfect but to novices.' The ideal is a perfect

union between the two, in which the whole man takes part, body, soul and spirit, like our Lord Jesus Christ, and some of the saints. Detached from the world and free from struggle and uncertainty, the soul gains a clarity and power before unknown to it. The feeling is keen, fervent and very pure. Detached from emotion and passion, the soul has power and light. The emotions obscure thought, but in this state thought is very clear. It is fully conscious and free – for the soul is never passive although it is freed from self engrossment and surrendered to God – it is in complete control and can either keep quite silent or pray actively. Sometimes the words of this prayer arise spontaneously from the heart and mind; sometimes there is deep silence. He contemplates with his whole self the divine uncreated light, the mysteries of the world and his own soul and body (St Isaac the Syrian quoted by Nil Skorski, *Testament spirituel sur la vie des Skits*).

All true prayer, that is prayer made in humility and surrender to God, is sooner or later quickened by the grace of the Holy Spirit. This grace becomes the force behind every action and thus everything in life. It ceases to be an activity and becomes our very being, the presence in us of him who fills all things and leads them to their own fulness.

BIBLIOGRAPHY

La Petite Philocalie du coeur translated and edited by J. Gouillard. Published in the series 'Le Livre de Vie', Editions du Seuil, Paris.

The Mystical Theology of the Eastern Church by Vladimir Lossky. Published by James Clarke, London and Allenson, Napierville, Illinois.

Living Prayer by Metropolitan Anthony. Published by Darton, Longman and Todd, London and Templegate, Springfield, Illinois.

School for Prayer (published in USA as *Beginning to Pray*) by Metropolitan Anthony. Published by Darton, Longman and Todd, London and The Paulist Newman Press, New York.

God and Man by Metropolitan Anthony. Published by Darton, Longman and Todd, London and the Paulist Newman Press, New York.

Techniques et Contemplation by A. Blum. Published in *Etudes Carmélitaines*, 1948 pp. 49-67.

The way of a Pilgrim translated by R. M. French. Revised edition published by SPCK, London with a foreword by Metropolitan Anthony.

Part II

Lord Stay With Us

by

Georges LeFebvre osb

CONTENTS

Introduction

LORD STAY WITH US

'He was probably right, the teacher who once told me that everyone has a mysterious prayer within him and does not know where it comes from, but that it presses everyone to pray however he can and in the way he knows.' Russian pilgrim.

TODAY PEOPLE ARE sometimes uneasy about the traditional forms of piety because they consider them too 'individualistic'. Is the ambiguity of the word partly responsible? What turns us in on ourselves is individualistic and shuts us off from other people. This is an essential contradiction to the christian mystery, the mystery of that union beginning in the Trinity and expressed in the one body of Christ whose members we all are, and of one another. So Mgr Elchinger could tell the Vatican Council: 'Individualism is a heresy.'

In the image of the Persons of the Trinity, each of whom is all that he is in relationship with the other two, a person is made for relationship with others and this is the only way he or she can develop. Turning inwards individualistically is isolation; we become persons in relationship with others.

But we can only truly turn to others by turning to God. In him alone can our relationships with others reach their proper depth.

To love others, and to respect them as that love requires, we must recognise their special relationship with God. God calls each single person and puts desire in his heart, that desire for God which is each man's truth and proper stature. But before we can see this in others, we must find it in ourselves.

To believe in this presence of God in all human life without being put off by appearances we must have experienced with amazement the faithfulness of God's love for us, however unfaithful we have been. We must have learnt how steadfast is God's love to us in our poverty, the love for humanity to whom he gave his Son.

If we wish to see our neighbour as we should, we must see him as he is in the eyes of God. Only then can we love him. This is why it is necessary to see ourselves in the eyes of God.

Then we can love with that love which comes from Christ. A love which is 'different' from all human goodwill, because we respect our neighbour for his relationship with Christ, even if he does not know it, because Christ knows every man. He is present in all our lives.

Thus we can be witnesses to the love of Christ by recognising his presence in our love. We are witnesses to the love of Christ and must bear witness to the joy he brings us: the joyful freedom of believing in this love and following where it leads untroubled by any care for self, free of self. A joy and a freedom making us available to others.

'We must have in us the almost careless spontaneity of a man dazzled by God,' which requires a living faith, 'and such faith requires the habit of recollection and paying attention to God' (François Stoop, Taizé Brother).

To bear witness to Christ and help others to recognise him and come to him, we need above all to live with him and stay with him. This is what we call prayer. What is prayer and how do we pray?

Christians who want to make prayer the centre of their lives often say they want texts not only explaining what prayer is, but texts to pray with. This is what the following pages try to be. They suggest certain prayerful attitudes in the presence of God. This is why they are often repetitive, returning to the same thoughts under different aspects, to try and come closer to God's mystery and live by it.

I

Never Alone

LOSING ONESELF

PRAYER IS AN end to isolation. It is living our daily life with someone. With him who alone can deliver us from solitude. For he is the only one we can find in our own heart, the only one to whom we can tell everything that is in us. He is ever present. Intimately. Prayer makes us aware of his presence, which we might not realise if we did not pay attention.

It is a living presence. The presence of him from whom we receive everything. We depend on him fundamentally. We discover his presence within us as we become aware of our total dependence on him. That is why prayer must be an attitude of humility. Not self regarding humility intent on considering our poverty and weakness. But a God-regarding humility joyful because of his closeness.

St Teresa of Avila writes in her 8th Spiritual discourse that she feels she has 'partly lost herself'. Doesn't anyone feel this who truly prays? He who does not pray belongs to himself. He is his own territory. He enjoys his independence. He is responsible for himself and he tries to reach his goal by his own efforts. He who prays knows that he needs another. Gradually he realises how much he needs this other to whom he turns in prayer, how he cannot live without him, how he can belong to none other but him who is his whole life. He is radically dispossessed of himself. He feels he has 'partly lost himself', he is not his own as he used to be, his treasure belongs to someone else.

Everything in him is now open to another, available to another and waiting on him. And in this openness to another, he gives up his independence, only to find true freedom: freedom of believing in a love which expects everything and to which he admits he owes everything. At the centre of prayer there must be faith in that love which created us for itself and which does its own work in us, which satisfies the desire it has given us. So our prayer does not belong to us. We have only our faith in that love which will not disappoint us however badly we serve. However poor and weak we are, our faith remains. It does not matter that we have nothing because this love is a love which can give us everything. It is present and at work in our secret hearts. We look towards it. It is the reason for our hope. We cannot even desire without it, our desires are so poor and weak. We can only wait for the Lord to work in us. 'Come and help me, because I am alone and I have only you O Lord' (Esther's prayer).

A COMMUNION

Praying is living our whole life as a communion with the Lord. Do we really understand what this means? For the other remains other to us, how ever close we are. In a true communion we come so close to the other that we are identified; it is more important for us for him to be what he is than for us to be what we are. We need him more than ourselves in order to be ourselves. A true relationship between persons cannot be an external bond which does not change them. A true personal relation-

ship enables two people to enter into each other without
losing their identity.

This can help us understand the communion between
the three persons of the Trinity. And it shows us that
there can be no true personal relationships without God
or without reference to God, the awareness of being in
him and through him. Personal relationships are such
a deep reality that they can only come from God. We
know a spiritual being by communion with it, by being
in one another. We know God by being aware of him in
ourselves. This is why prayer is essentially personal. Grace
cannot be impersonal. It is the acceptance of someone.
Someone with whom we live, who has a plan for us
and who himself fulfils it patiently, perseveringly and
with faithful love.

God exists before us. Prayer does not create his
presence, it makes us aware of it. How freely we live in
this presence if we truly believe in it. It makes itself felt
in little ways, which are not proof but rather an invitation to turn towards it. We must believe, and be led to
believe more and more simply and express this belief
by an attitude of submission.

It is less important to become aware of this presence
than to accept it. We have to accept that it holds us and
we no longer belong to ourselves. This is the free consent
of love. We consent to be in and through another.

IN OUR HUMBLE CONDITION

God came to us in the Incarnation by coming to share
our condition. It is in this human condition that he is
present to us and that we live with him. We have to
learn to recognise the divine mystery which he shares
with us in the human form it takes in us. We must not
seek 'beyond' ourselves. It is *in* ourselves that the change
has happened through the presence of the Lord, our
belief in this presence and attention to it. We are recon-

ciled, freed. Everything acquires a profounder meaning,
a density. We cry to God with all that is deepest and
truest in us. That is why this aspiration is different from
all our other ones. We encounter God in all that is deepest in ourselves. We are not astonished by the darkness
of God's mystery, we simply accept it, although we do
not see plain. We do not know what power of love we
are opening to when we do this. If we saw clearly
we would be aware of the presence of God simply by
being aware of ourselves, because in his presence we are
all that we are. Nothing in us, nothing in the very
depths of our hearts can live without him. Our awareness of his presence makes us naturally obedient to it.

We must live our whole lives in his presence, realising
that we do not belong to ourselves but to his love. We
are in his hands, confidently. Simply and with spontaneous joy. However little we know of our own hearts,
there is something in us which looks towards God and
his grace. We must simply offer it to him. We must know
that he holds us in his hands. We must do what he
wants. We must let him lead us, form us, make us do his
will. He does not manifest his presence by any clear sign,
but we know that we cannot live without him. Our bond
with him always remains. However empty, wretched and
dull we feel, the Lord is present in us and at work. We
must believe in his presence and trust him. We must
let him take over.

We must let the Lord accomplish his work in us
in the way he chooses, for he alone can do it. We must
accept everything as coming from him. We must believe
simply and joyfully in his presence, for we cannot doubt
his love. We must let the joy of his presence calm us.
For his love cannot fail.

2

Humble Love

IN FAITH

OUR PRAYER EXPRESSES much more than we are
conscious of. It is an attachment and consent to be what
we are in Christ. Our whole being is involved. Our true
being is a gift of God in Christ, in communion with
him. We should accept it as a gift. We should live in that
freedom which is the recognition of that gift of love by
which we are all that we are. We should see everything
that happens to us in the light of our life in Christ,
then we will understand it properly. We should accept it
meekly, believing and accepting the mystery. What we
are in Christ is hidden from us, but we come to it by an
act of faith, which is contained in the faith of the Church.
We find our unfailing support in the faith of the church,
with which we are in communion.

In the light of this faith we can grasp what our heart
guesses at, and live by it through all manner of
adversity. We should bear humble witness to what the
Lord works in us. He allows us to guess and glimpse his
will. This affirmation of faith makes it a support, a com-
fort and a joy, something deep within us which remains
the first essential even when everything seems empty.
This firm faith in God gives us a freedom towards everything else; in his presence it seems essentially relative.
A joyful freedom. Even when everything seems empty

we can be certain that the Lord is there. He cannot fail us, however badly we fail. We must live simply with this certainty. And we will realise more and more the truth of his presence. We will feel the joy of his presence.

We know that someone is there and we know what that someone means to us. Christ is present in peace – he fulfils our deepest wish – and that peace is our faith in him. This is where we must seek him. This is where we may abide with him. In difficulty we do not have to accept 'something' which costs us dearly, but to let ourselves be led by 'someone' in love and trust. We must follow obediently where he leads.

BE HUMBLE 'WITH' GOD

Faith is recognition of the mystery, surrendering our-selves to its fulness. Faith is humility. The Lord is present at the heart of all humility. We can feel the truth of this by living it. With the silence of humble attention, respect, and a sense of the infinite fulness of God. Humility feels itself in deep harmony with this fulness. And in this harmony it slowly finds that the fulness is also a mystery of humility, a loving God.

We must not only be humble 'before' God. But more fundamentally, we must be humble 'with' God who comes to us in a mystery which is a mystery of humility. We have no other God but Christ. Everything that we know about God through revelation, we know in and through the humanity of Christ. 'He who has seen me has seen the father' (Jn. 14.9.).

Christ in all his words and deeds is our God living and doing, fully himself. Our God is he who is humble merci-ful, weak among men, suffering with them. He is Christ among us, with us. He is the God whose omnipotence is expressed in the mystery of the Cross, the mystery of humility, poverty, weakness by which he shows the ful-ness of his love which is stronger than us, defeats our resistance and overcomes our sin. He is personally involved in a loving relationship with us. He lives with us, in our condition.

As he once shared our human condition on earth, now he still shares it in each of us. Through his love he truly shares our life. In love it is impossible to stay apart, love demands life together, involvement, solidarity. He lives with our poverty and wretchedness in this solidarity of love. He does not cast a merciful glance at us from afar. He joins us on our way and his mercy shares our poverty and our whole life.

We should also see others as living thus with Christ. We should respect the presence of Christ in their everyday life. We should love even their failings, for Christ is also present in them. This is the source of that patience which is also love. Humility is the ultimate secret of God's perfection, because it is the fulness and delicacy of his love. A humble God, infinitely close. In the sight of God's humility, only humility makes sense. A humble God, found simply but very close in our secret prayer.

The Lord is infinitely beyond us, but also infinitely close. That is why his presence can be both secret and intimate. We must be content with nothing less than God, but we must find him in our simplest, humblest and most unassuming prayer. We must be humble before God who calms and satisfies all our desire. We can look to God quite simply, but we put our whole self into this relation. We only exist through it.

NEEDING ANOTHER

Loving is not just looking at someone, it is living with him. It is sharing our life and all our reasons for living with another, sharing even our self awareness. It is becoming inseparable. Loving is forming a bond so close, that our inmost being would change if the other ceased to exist. We can no longer see ourselves except in terms of this other. So we truly no longer belong to ourselves. We are radically stripped bare of our self possession because we know that everything we are is in relation to another, in communion with him. There is nothing left but this presence.

This presence can be obscure but it must either remain our deepest truth or we perish. We cannot live otherwise. Our poverty is so radical that it must be a cry to God. God cannot be purely and simply absent. Our poverty itself speaks of him and he dwells in it.

Praying is keeping away from all those things where we do not find what we seek. We are waiting, appealing for him who can satisfy us. We turn towards him. We live in vital need of him. We are open to him. We cry for what will one day satisfy our heart and is already present in hope. We can now only guess at the fulness for which we are made, and our desire for it. Our openness to God is a grace, a gift. We should accept it as such and live with it, in simplicity. We are barely aware of it, we wait. However it is by this gift that we are all that we are. It is our one deep truth. The gift of living in prayer is one with the gift we shall receive of living in heaven. It is the same living reality and the seed contains the fruit. So our humble prayer contains within it a hidden fulness. The only worthy praise of God is our whole being involved in communion with him and only living in and through this loving communion. This is the joy of being filled by God, turned towards God.

3

Learning to Believe

HE WHO LOVES US

THE MEANING OF our time of trial here below is not to give us the chance to earn a reward but to teach us how to love, to enable us to enter into a true loving relationship with God, in which our response to him is a truly personal free response. If God keeps us in the dark, this is not because he wishes to keep his distance from us, it is in order to lead us to a deeper communion with himself through humility.

We must trust in the Lord. Let him act. He can use the darkness to lead us further into the mystery of his presence. All that his presence is for us can be expressed in a simple attitude of waiting. We cry to someone, who is not far off, but is himself present in our cry. He is there and he holds us. His presence is more powerful than the darkness. Praying is to live in the sight of him who by his love makes us what we are. We must be obedient to him. We cry to the Lord who lives in the depths of our heart and who is one with our deepest being. We have only to listen to him. It is like listening to silence. A silent cry, simple, peaceful, an act of faith.

This cry is not only the deepest desire of our heart but an answer to the gift of God which is beyond the imagination of our heart. Everything we find at the depths of our heart shows us how we are loved. We must have faith in this cry and live by it, through all the silences. Our peace and our confidence are supported by our faith in the love of Christ. We must truly believe in it. Our one deep need, without which we cannot live must be to feel ourselves in harmony with Christ.

We must be everything that we are in an act of faith – which is putting our whole self into the hands of him who is our sole reason for living. Prayer is what makes all the difference. We would not be the same if we did not have in our heart the awareness of being in the hands of God. We must pay attention to God, not just in thought, but more deeply, with our whole self. This attitude is quite simple and the Lord will see our deep desire to be available to him, our turning to him, our humble hope. We must believe in the power of the mystery of grace which holds us and only care about giving ourselves and opening ourselves as much as we can. We should feel close to anyone who has not yet received the gift of faith but is still in the hands of God whom he seeks without knowing it. The mystery is a living reality. It is present and manifest in human history, in the lives of our neighbours and our own. It is Christ present and active in the power of his Spirit in all humanity and all time. Everything subsists in him and through him. He surrounds us.

THE HUMILITY OF FAITH

The humility of faith is true humility, a simple poverty. It is an ordinary poverty. Humility is the only way we can express our littleness, our powerlessness in the sight of God. The sign that we are in the presence of God may be a deep peace, but also a deep humility. And perhaps the humility will lead us to the peace.

When we no longer even desire, it is enough that we know that someone has a plan for us and to agree to this plan. We can only live by an act of trust which we con-

stantly renew and this makes us realise our closeness
to him who is our only hope. Living in this state of trust
and radical dependence makes us lose ourselves. Everything in our lives belongs to God and God alone. Nothing
belongs to us any more. The work he gives us to do, he
does through us. We must let him do everything he
pleases. We must belong wholly to the Lord and we will
become more and more aware of him the more we trust
him and understand the meaning of our act of faith
by which we give ourselves to him. Our act of faith
brings us into closer and closer communion with Christ.
We discover the meaning of our faith by living it in self
surrender. We discover what Christ means to us and
what it means to put our hope in him.

Life is given to us to learn to believe. Everything
that happens, however upsetting, should lead us further
in our faith. Whatever our difficulties and our fears of
going astray, we can be sure that we are on the right
road if we understand more and more clearly what faith
means. The Lord does his work in us. Awareness of our
poverty is a taste of the infinite fulness whose presence
makes us feel our poverty. And even in our poverty we
can put complete trust in this fulness. Our trust in God's
love must also be trust in his mercy. We must accept his
plan which is his mercy. We must see our poverty in the
sight of his mercy. And we must also judge others
in this mercy's sight. Then nothing can prevent us loving.
This is the true christian attitude. This is the only way we
can look to God with confidence and live simply and
freely in that confidence.

WITH CHRIST

We must have faith in the mystery of our life in Christ,
that communion with him constantly renewed in the
eucharist which can become a familiar and ever present
reality in our lives. What was Christ's own consciousness

of his sonship? Did he not also in this share to some
extent in our human weakness? We have only an imperfect knowledge, proper to our earthly state, of our own
deep truth, what we are through our communion with
Christ. Didn't he come close enough to us for us to be
able to feel that in this imperfection he is also with
us? That this also makes us members of him and we can
live it in him?

We become aware of what we are in Christ by sharing his trusting submission to the Father's will: 'My food
is to do the will of him that sent me and to accomplish
his work' (Jn. 4.34.). Our human condition is essentially
a conditon of distress. We must accept this. But we are
given someone to hope in. We are given Christ.

4

Knowing We Are Loved

AN AMAZING LOVE

OUR PRAYER BECOMES truly simple, the more we understand that God alone does his own work in us. Then simple silence becomes an attitude of faith and humility. We look simply towards him from whom we await everything. We realise the extent of our dependence the more we grow in simplicity. We know how poor we are, we ourselves and all those things that we are incapable of giving up but let us still offer God our sincere desire that he should take what we do not know how to give and let us be peaceful. We belong to God, we are in his hands. This is the ground of our hope. Nothing can destroy this hope because it is beyond earthly hope. We should be amazed that God loves us. How could such an amazing love fail us? We should have the humility to see that our wretchedness, however great, cannot be an obstacle to the power of God.

Everything we have comes from God. He willed us and made us what we are. Our deepest being is an expression of what God means us to be: it is creative grace by which he forms us according to his plan. His loving plan. Everything in us is caught up in this grace. Everything in us comes from this grace and it is present in all things.

Christ takes hold of our desires and takes them up into

his grace. We must learn to recognise him at the heart of our desires, because he alone can satisfy them. We must hope, with all simplicity.

LOVING IS BELONGING

We must experience ourselves as belonging to someone else. We may be poor or sinful but we can remember quite simply that we belong to God who is our deep truth. He is our cure. We must accept that we cannot be sure of ourselves. In this insecurity our one hope is faith in the love of God whose mercy is infinite. We must remain 'alone with this God by whom we know we are loved and forget ourselves' (St Teresa of Avila). We must believe in the love of God and its reliability. We know that we are in his hands and that he will not fail us. However feebly we pray, he will not fail us. To believe in the love of God is to pray. Our prayer does not rely on what we are in God's sight but on our faith in what he is to us, unfailingly. We can become simple in the spiritual life to the extent that we truly believe in the love of God – a mystery which is beyond us whose fulness is our boundless hope. God is close to us, he really shares his life with us in true communion. Isn't this amazing? How can we understand it except as infinite love – God's humility which is ready to bring his greatness into a truly loving relationship with our smallness.

THE SIMPLICITY OF FAITH

The great God can only truly reveal himself in simplicity. We should not be more astonished by the simplicity of prayer than by the simplicity of bread and wine which he has given us as signs of his presence. This simplicity has something essential to teach us about God and about the relationship he wants to have with us. Very simple attitudes: humility, a sense of our poverty, confidence, inner peace, the feeling that we are not alone. They are indeed simple attitudes but they have a density and depth which go beyond themselves, towards something which our heart wants but which is greater than our hearts.

These attitudes have no meaning except in the light of faith and are also the expression of our truest being. To live them is to live the reality of our faith and to become conscious of it as an experienced reality. What God tells us in Christ and what we hear from the Church in our communion with the faith of the church is not merely an answer to the prayer of our heart. Our prayer has become what it is in the light of this faith. It is penetrated by this faith. It enables us to live by this faith. It may be sure or unsure. We may not understand it but we know that it is there.

It lies so deep in us that we may not be aware of it. We live by it. It is a call for God's presence or perhaps, more than we know, the joy of being gladdened by his presence. It is such a deep experience that it remains through all silences and darkness. Silence, our inner silence, just as it is. To remain in it is to remain with him who, we know, is always with us. When we know that someone is there, keeping silence is listening. 'What the soul does then is to practise what has been done in her, that is love continuing the union with God' (John of the Cross).

LOVE WHICH UNITES US

We know that we are loved in a deeply personal way and also in a way that takes complete possession of us. This is why we can believe in it. It is not a privilege setting us apart – or we should feel unworthy of it – it is a love which unites all of us. This love which is personal to each one of us is not confined to one or other of us. It is for others too. It is an aspect of the mystery by which we live

together in a communion whereby each of us is all that
he is – all that he is given to be – with and for the others
We belong to each other in love. This love makes us become an offering.

The Lord is present in the lives of each one of us. He
does his work in us with the infinite patience of his grace.
To judge our neighbour is to judge not him but his
relationship with Christ. It is to judge Christ's work in
him. We can be sure of one thing only: someone exists
upon whom we can always rely and who will never fail
us. No darkness can dismay us because it is merely a
sign of our own poverty. And this poverty itself bears
witness to him who alone can enrich it. We know that
the Lord is there and he can freely do his will in us. He
is all our hope, he is the answer, given in advance, to all
our prayer. God is faithful. We know that we are in his
hands. We must be willing to remain there. He is the
real desire of our heart. He is the answer. He shows us
his love for us. We do not know everything that is in
our hearts by which we live.

LOVE WHICH SATISFIES US

Our heart can only be satisfied by knowing that it lives
in a true communion with infinite love. When we know
this we feel the peace of knowing the truth. Our heart
bears witness to God's presence. However simple, quiet
and secret this presence may be, it expresses our certainty in faith and hope. Our desire is deeper than our
heart. It comes from further off. But we can guess at
God's love for us. Our need to love is also a mystery
because it makes us like God. We are created in his
image and likeness which is deeper than we know. We
have only to give our free consent, so that his measure-
less love can become the measure of our love for others
with whom we are in communion in him. We have found
someone who will never disappoint our love. We can

always love him more and find him more worthy of
love. Our hearts are satisfied.

LOVE WHICH SETS US FREE

God is present. To believe in his presence is to let it
become everything to us. A presence which is everything
to us and essentially secret. This double nature of his
presence shows us the sort of attention we should pay to
it. The more it means everything to us, the more there
will be something which is always there, whatever the
darkness, and we should never doubt it. Someone who
means everything to us, more deeply than we know. We
experience his presence in freedom and simplicity because it is the presence of someone who loves us. He is
with us and he makes us free, simple and without
desires. Because we know that we never have enough
faith in his love. 'With you I have no desire on earth'
(Ps. 72).

This love is candid, like a child's gaze or astonished
smile. It accepts the gift it is given without asking how
it came to be given. Its simplicity is its freedom. It is
free from all the complications and anxieties which
would make it turn back in on itself. We should humbly
find peace in the thought that it is God who sees us and
judges us. We should not think of God as someone who
'forbids' us satisfactions but as a love watching over us
and guiding us which we must follow confidently because it leads to that fulness which is our goal. We
should live in the sight of his loving kindness and recognise it in all that he asks of us.

We should be docile which is to let the Lord work in
us through events, through other people. We should let
him take in this way what we are so bad at giving. We
should be patient and have confidence in him. Our
prayer should express this docility. That is what it means
to be in the Lord's hands. That is prayer.

Living the presence of Christ is to want, think and feel everything with him. We can live very imperfect feelings with him if we genuinely want to improve. We learn to know him by meeting him in the Eucharist. He is always with us. He is in our heart and always says yes even when we say no.

5

Simplicity and Freedom

BOUNDLESS LOVE

WE CAN BE certain that a real joy exists and it is already present at the centre of our lives. Loving someone is being happy because of that person. Loving someone is knowing and saying with our whole self that this other person means everything to us. It is recognising that our self lives by another and only exists through that other. It is agreeing to be what we really are: a cry to God, an inability to live except in relation to him, in him, through him, with him. Loving God is not only recognising him as the answer to our prayer. That is a limited sort of love. It is only because God exists that we have this desire for him in us. He is the measure of this desire which is greater than our hearts. It is because God is infinitely lovable that we have an infinite need to love. This is not just a need we have. We are made for another person. Nothing in us makes sense except in relation to him. That is why our cry, our need has an absolute value.

We are grasped by the mystery of love. The only answer we can give is to believe in it, quite simply. We need a real humility to discover the fulness of communion with the love of God. Because this is a truthful attitude to him, it is the only way of recognising him as he really is. This will still be true when we see him in heaven. We must simply accept the poverty of our prayer and be peaceful. This is an act of faith in him who can do what he wants with our poverty. An act of faith – faith in someone – which engages our whole life. It is not our work. It is a gift. We can only see the signs which allow us to think we have received this gift, that we live by it. That is enough to make us grateful. What grace works in us, we live in freedom and simplicity, truly believing in its power upon our hearts. We must be open to this work of grace not try and somehow grab it.

God does not hide. We can always find signs of his presence just beyond us, so that we never cease to seek him. Prayer is the expression of what is deepest and thus most natural and spontaneous in us. It is one with our inmost nature, that by which we are most truly ourselves. That is why we can live by it without noticing. Whatever the ways by which the Lord leads us in prayer, as in all our lives, they are always his ways and the important thing is to know what is the right attitude so that we can do what he wants. This in one form or another is always an attitude of humility. God loves us. He knows us. He knows our weakness. He is moved to see that however keenly we are aware of our poverty and sinfulness, we do not despair or give up seeking him because we need his love too much.

UNITED BY GOD'S LOVE

God loves us quite freely. He does not love in our way and with our limits. He loves in his own divine way, with his fulness, generosity and freedom. He has no limits. Thus we should receive him and let him fill us. We should trust and think no more of our poverty and then we will begin to understand the meaning of his love. His love is not enclosed by our limits and it does not stop at whom I might love 'less' God loves with the same love us. He loves everybody and this unites us. The brother

that he has for me. Our daily relationship must be lived
in the presence of him who loves us both together.

IN THE LIGHT OF FAITH

Humility and trust, humility and joy are all one in our
relationship with God upon whom we depend totally. We
are in the presence of his love. We cannot of course
express this faith properly, it is beyond words. However it is not totally cut off from all that we can express
by words. But what our words say about faith slowly
becomes a living reality. This is our life, and truly our
light. By it we live in the presence of God and become
inseparable from him. So praying is simply living, being
ourselves as grace has formed us. Praying is letting ourselves be drawn to the deepest desire of our hearts, to
what is truest in us, and not being distracted from it.

Faith is a gift which comes from him in whom we
believe. He arouses it in us and puts in our heart something greater than our heart. Faith would not be possible if he in whom we believe did not exist. Faith bears
witness to him. It has its own certainty beyond all our
certainties and all our doubts. The love to which we have
given our faith, he who is our hope and joy, is not an
unknown God, invisible and far away. It is Christ whom
we see speaking and acting in the Gospel and whom we
encounter in the Eucharist. 'He who has seen me has
seen the Father' (Jn. 14.9.).

If we are united with Christ in a personal closeness –
the sign of this is our encounter with him in the
Eucharist – if we live with him in a relationship which
makes us someone to him, this means we want above all
to agree with him in everything. Christ is present. If we
truly believe in him. If he really means everything to us,
we have only to look to his presence, not to ourselves.
Christ is our hope. His presence in our lives is a promise
that none of our desires will remain unsatisfied. He gives

us peace. Whether we feel this peace or not, he has given us the gift of believing in it. Believing is to accept a truth in faith, however little we see what it means. Believing is experience because it involves our deepest being.

6

Lord I Have No One But You

CHRIST IS GOD present to humanity, to all human history. We are as sure of his presence in each of our lives as we are sure of his presence in human history. We should live this certainty in all simplicity, because it is the object of our faith. If we truly believe in the presence of Christ, if it truly means everything to us, we have only to look to him. We should not keep analysing our attitude to God. We should not keep looking at ourselves but should look at him. We should simply remain in his presence. In his presence we are changed as we ought to change. We should offer ourselves to the Lord in all our poverty with nothing but our desire to obey him and to let him work in us.

We are in the presence of him who knows what he wants of us. If we can only stammer in his sight, he can understand what we are trying to say, what we want and how to give it to us. This our utter dependence on him is a great mystery of love. We know that someone is present in our lives and at work in us. We must pay attention to him but his action goes beyond our poor weak attention, which is so easily distracted, so easily disconcerted. Our attention itself is the work of the preceding grace, which arouses it and which is not limited by it.

We should not try and open ourselves more to the love of God by feeling a more intense desire. We should simply offer him our desire, our need for him, just as it is, perhaps barely expressed, as an act of humble trust. Our feelings remain our own simple human feelings. The fact that they are feelings for God is shown simply by a certain depth and peace. Prayer is looking towards God who is inseparable from our lives. In our prayer we express everything in our lives which is a cry for God, a real desire for him. This living reality is the foundation of our prayer. It directs our hearts spontaneously towards God and keeps our inner silence in his presence.

A MERCIFUL LOVE

The sign that prayer leads us deeper into the mystery of God's love is that it gives us a deeper sense of his mercy. First of all our prayer itself has need of mercy. We make our humble efforts in the sight of this mercy for the Lord is always with us. Even when we feel that we are only wretched sinners in God's sight, fit only for reprimand and punishment, this can still be a loving relationship if we accept it humbly. If we get into the habit of seeing our neighbour in the light of the mystery of love and mercy which surrounds us all, this leads us to have a right attitude towards him. We can no longer doubt the mystery. To be patient and merciful is to recognise humbly that we ourselves need mercy.

If our hearts are filled with the presence of Christ so that we really live with his own love, we can at least begin to see how this love is stronger than everything and can never grow weary. So our own hearts will become gentler and more peaceful in the warmth of this love. We must let his grace grow gradually stronger. We must allow it to work and not put obstacles in its way, we must be on the same side as grace and not on the side of our own rebellious feelings however strong these may be and however feeble we may feel our control over them. We must be patient and confident.

With each of our brothers we are in the presence of God's mystery, the mystery of his infinitely patient grace, the mystery of what it can do in each one of us, in spite of all our failings. We must respect this mystery.

We must not judge our neighbour, for our reactions are always so imperfect and even if we cannot see things as Christ sees them, we should at least try and have Christ's attitudes and the joy of agreeing with him. Instead of living with our neighbours immersed in the petty difficulties of daily life we should try to see them in the light of the mystery of love which surrounds us all. Then it will be easy for us to live in our prayers the mystery whose sign is given to us every day in the Eucharist and which is thus always with us. If our act of faith is really an act of love for Christ in complete confidence and humility, this faith will always prevail and we shall see all things in its light, and first of all our neighbour. For it is faith in someone who remains the same through all our changeability, for he does not change.

AN INFINITE LOVE

In our prayer we are really in the presence of a God whose greatness is his love which has infinite resources to draw us to him and bring us close to him. He must be able to love us in our wretchedness in order to be able to cure us. Everything poor and dark in our cry to God pays homage in its own fashion to the mystery of God. We should never be amazed at our poverty in the sight of God. We must accept that we do not even know whether we truly love, that we have only a very halting sort of love to offer him. We must have faith in Christ in whom we find new strength to cope with fresh difficulties and darkness. The more we realise that we are in the Lord's presence and the peace of his presence, the readier we shall be to obey him and let his will rule ours and speak through ours. Believing that someone is holding us in his hands is letting ourselves be guided by him. It does not mean that we feel his presence bodily. It is being drawn to an attitude of obedience. His presence is a mystery. The deeper we penetrate into this mystery the more simply we are able to accept it. We must not be astonished by our own poor response, but open our hearts in faith to what we constantly receive. The deeper we enter into the mystery, the better we understand how it is present in our lives in a simple and unspectacular way. 'My son you are always with me (I am always with you) all that is mine is thine' (Lk. 15.31.). This is the truth by which we live in prayer. The whole fulness and power of God's love for us is present in our cry for him which he himself puts in us. We must trust his love and believe in him. Turning towards God means first of all living in his sight. Living in God's presence and looking to him does not mean we think of him as far away and remain just as we are before him. It is to enter into a communion with him, in which he transforms us in his image and makes us like him.

HE WHO IS EVERYTHING TO US

Loving means that the person we love is everything to us. As Christ becomes our true reason for living we know that we truly love him and we live in the joy of this love. Let this joy enfold all our life and be so strong that nothing can change it or allow us to forget it. It is enough to satisfy us for always and we can lack nothing. We are sure of the love of Christ because he cannot disappoint us and he will give us the grace not to disappoint him.

Our love of God is deeper than our awareness of it. It is a reality of grace which we live in the darkness of

faith. We should gratefully recognise this love in our
hearts as the gift of the Holy Spirit who cannot be confined to our limitations. All our weakness and meanness
does not prevent the Lord from seeing what in us is still
a cry for him. He takes it up in his grace and he stays
with us. However poor and empty we are, we are not
alone. Because it is taken into the grace of his
presence our poverty itself is a cry to God. Not something that comes from us, a feeling we feel and on which
we can rely, but it is the living certainty of a presence,
of him who bears us in his hands. We must believe in
this presence and put all our hope in it. We belong to
God. We must give our whole hearted consent to this.
Perhaps we can never do this perfectly. But we must take
great care not to abandon it.

We cannot adequately express our knowledge of a person, what he means to us. We must live our knowledge.
It is the same with Christ and his presence in our lives
if he is really a person to us, if we 'know' him. He first
of all 'knows' us. For he has always been with us and his
love has never grown weary. His presence is secret and
discreet. We should recognise in his secret presence the
sign of his mysterious fulness and see it as an invitation
to trust him totally. We should humbly receive the gift
of his presence, and accept that it should remain silent
and secret. We can expect everything from it if we lose
ourselves in its sight. Before him it is impossible not to
be simple. The more we feel ourselves to be in his
presence, the more transparent we feel. We can be
confident and hope for everything from him because we
trust in him, expecting nothing from our own poverty.

HUMBLE CONFIDENCE

We should have a simple desire to offer to him who can
satisfy it. A desire that is greater than our heart. We can
guess at it beyond what we are conscious of. And if we

find that we do not know whether we really want what remains so dark, we can be confident in him who calls us to him. We must simply desire what he invites us to hope for in an act of faith in him alone. By turning towards him we will find a remedy for all our ills. We belong to another. We should efface ourselves before him. This attitude is so profoundly true that everything out of harmony with it appears as an illusion. Even if there is only emptiness and silence, we can feel something which is truer than anything which we might be tempted to seek for to fill it. We have a presentiment of God's love for us and call to us. We feel a joy which is a grace we should open our hearts to. We should live by it freely without looking at it too much, without wanting to take 'possession' of it. We should accept it from moment to moment as a gift. We should cling silently to what is at the heart of our self awareness and also beyond it: the living reality of our relationship with God. We must agree with the direction of our will, our whole being, towards God. And we must live this in reality.

BE OBEDIENT

It is an act of humility towards the mystery of the presence of the Lord in our lives to accept trials and difficulties, even upsetting ones, even ones which come from other people. It is letting the Lord follow his plan for us and respecting the mystery of his presence. We must let the Lord be quite free to follow his plan for us. We must accept everything and everybody he uses to fulfil this plan. When it is impossible for us not to be sad, our sadness should be gentle and serene. We must accept suffering and not become bitter.

We must not worry about all that is human and weak in us but we must learn to recognise the Lord's presence in the midst of our difficulties and trials. We must have confidence in him. This confidence is our consent to him,

our renunciation of everything which might stand in the
way of his grace. When someone makes us suffer, we
should not be annoyed for this is always an unworthy
attitude, we should try rather to discover how to behave
in such a way as to help our tormentor to improve. We
must go to God together. The love of God is present in
a communion, which we can only enter by loving all who
share in it. We should love them as they are, and see
God's love in them. We should recognise the Lord who
is testing us by this means and we should see both ourselves and the person who hurts us in the mystery of his
mercy. This means we must not be hostile. Humility
towards God must be part of our deepest being. In our
prayer and in our whole life we should not want to
achieve something which would be our own work, we
should not try and stand alone. We must believe in him
who has taken us into his hands and who lovingly does
his own work in us. He leads us gradually to become the
person he can love, the person who has his own unique
place in the communion of love which he invites us to
enter. We must believe in his presence and live by the
grace of his presence.

We must allow the Lord to make us gentler. We must
not become hardened in obstinacy. We must try and find
the point where our self love should give way so that
we can find peace again. The Lord does what he wants
with us. He leads us wherever he wants. We should not
try and resist him. Let him form us.

Thy will be done. This is freedom.

THE SILENCE OF FAITH

We must not lose faith in what we cannot see. The silence
of faith. Respect for this mystery. The mystery of someone who loves us. He gives us everything. We must remain open to him, in expectation. We feel that we are
satisfied. The Lord satisfies us all. Know this. Know that

he loves us. Believe because we cannot doubt Christ, his presence in the world and thus in each one of us. His love for the world and so for each one of us. We are taken up in this great mystery. We should simply believe in it. Our faith should be plain faith. Faith is poverty. It accepts certainty as a gift which brings it peace. Emptiness and darkness can always be felt as poverty and become an attitude of confidence. In the most humble prayer we find peace. And we know there is no other way. Anything else would lead to a dead end. God loves us with a love beyond our conception. In the presence of this mystery we can only stammer. But in spite of our poverty, we do have, perhaps more than we realise, a true apprehension of this love. This is expressed by the simplicity of our confidence in God and our meek acceptance of our poverty.

Even when we no longer know it we are loved by a love which never ceases. We must let it work. Let it do what it wants with us. We should sincerely want to be open to the Lord, pliable in his hands. He sees our desire even when we cannot express it. Our desire can only have one object: what God wants of us. We must believe that he wants it with all the strength and power of his love. Let him accomplish his work in our weakness, in spite of our weakness. Expect him peacefully. We can only live in a free consent – the humble wish to be obedient to the Lord's will. Our silence should be an acceptance, the sign of our availability. We should open ourselves to God's love in simplicity, recognising that all we have comes from him, that his omnipotence alone is working in us. This is a truthful attitude towards God's love.

KNOWING WE ARE LOVED

We know we are loved. The only proper reply to this love is to ask it to take all that we do not know how to give. If the Lord is truly our joy and our peace, if we truly cannot live without him, we always feel within us something of that peace that comes from him. The depths of our hearts belong to him. He knows this. Abandoning ourselves in God's hands cannot be a grand gesture. We can only do it simply, like a child. Then it is true confidence. This is the candour and freshness of true confidence, a confidence lived in humility, poverty and detachment. It is the source of serene patience. If we humbly recognise our poverty, the Lord must have pity on us. We must truly believe not in an abstract mercy but in someone whose mercy we know by experience and who will lead us where he wants if we do not absolutely refuse.

Our heart should become one with the love that is its life, so that this is the only love it knows and it sees everyone in the light of this love. Believing in the love of God is being gentle to all those he loves. When God's light reveals to us what our lives have been, we will not be disappointed. We will be cured of the illusion of measuring things according to our own measure, when they are beyond measure.

7

The Gift of God's Presence

WE KNOW THAT we are in the presence of God. If we behave accordingly we gradually become more aware of God's presence. We remain silent in his presence because we know that we are not alone. This is an act of faith in his presence. When everything goes wrong for us, we should not seek in ourselves something to lean on, but we should affirm our faith in God's presence. We should stand quite simply in his prseence; he knows what is in the depths of our heart. We should simply look towards God without being self conscious about it. We should simply be what we are, as God has made us, in his sight. We are what we are because God's love for us is what it is. He has made us what we are because of the unique personal relationship he wishes to have with us. We only exist in and through this love. It takes hold of our inmost being. We should give it the freedom to do what it wants with us.

Our confidence and humble submission is far short of what it would be if we really knew what God's love for us was. But we should simply offer ourselves as we are, knowing all our shortcomings, for this is the only adequate response to his love. God loves us and does not ever forget us. He can turn anything in us into a prayer

if it remains turned towards him, even if we are not
aware of it. We remain before the Lord in silence. We
can be content that he knows that our hearts cannot live
without him. In God's eyes, by the very fact that he looks
at us we become what he loves. Christ works in us all
through our life by the constant presence of his grace
and the faithfulness of his love. He puts his mark on us
more indelibly than we are aware. He makes our hearts
live by him and unable to live without him. He puts a
prayer in the depths of our being. We become aware of
the work of grace in us by trying to be more faithful
to it and to live by it in our behaviour towards our neighbours. We are taken up into the infinite fulness of a
mystery of love. It is this love which should pour out of
our hearts towards our neighbours. It should overcome
all obstacles. Nothing can be for us a reason for loving
less.

RESPECT FOR THE MYSTERY

We should have a deep wish to be faithful to God's plan
for us and to respond to his love. A desire in faith. A
desire which is an act of faith. A desire which comes not
from us and which is not limited to our own capacities.
We cannot give a full account of it. Faith is firstly the
apprehension of a mystery too great for us to understand. We believe in a truth which is beyond all our own
truths. The only proper attitude is to remain before it
in silence, in humility and adoration. We should truly
accept the poverty of our prayer and believe that with
the freedom of his grace the Lord works what he wants
in our humility. It does not matter if we have little to
offer in our prayer, so long as we offer it humbly. However poor our prayer may be, it is still prayer if it stays
humble. It is an act of faith in the immense mystery of
love in which we are involved, the bowing down of our
whole self before it. In our weakness we must live a

mystery infinitely beyond us but also intimately present to us.

We want our prayer to be in some way a grasp of God's mystery, recognition of the mystery and of our own littleness before it. We should accept the poverty of our prayer, our emptiness and put our trust in God finding all our support in the mysterious fulness of his love. Prayer is not like a place which belongs to us, where we are at home and at ease. We must accept homelessness and total poverty and learn constantly to receive from moment to moment prayer as a gift. We should have an accepting attitude, open to him who, we know is there even if he gives no sign of his presence. Our situation is always precarious but we can be confident because we know we are loved.

When we receive the Eucharist we cannot doubt that the grace of this mystery is active in our darkness. Can we not then see that our darkness is not unbelief and in no way an obstacle or a refusal of grace? If we really had a sense of God, no darkness would appal us. It would simply lead us to surrender ourselves more completely.

GOD LOOKS ON US WITH LOVE

How can God not love those whom he has made unable to be happy without his love and to whom he has given this bond with him which is unbreakable even if they do not know it or go astray? And we too must love others as God loves them. The way God looks at those who truly seek him through all their weaknesses and errors, is a mystery. The more kindly we look on others, the deeper we enter into this mystery. We will always fall short of its fulness. God will always love more than we do.

God is present. We must believe in his presence and our faith is the result of all our life of grace. Believing that God loves us is to recognise what his love has meant

to us, what we have received from him. It is to believe
in what grace has done in the depths of our hearts, even
if it is not plain to see. The christian mystery is always
expressed in the reality of a history. Our prayer cannot
be reduced to what we feel or do not feel at the present
moment. It is the expression of what we have become
throughout the course of grace in our lives.

Recognising that we have received and continue to
receive everything from God is to recognise his love for
us in the work of grace in our hearts. How then can we
not want to open ourselves wholly to this love of God
and to remove all obstacles from its way? Believing in
God is believing that there is nothing in us which was
not made to be satisfied. It is trusting serenely in the
loving plan which created us.

TOTAL ACCEPTANCE

We must offer total acceptance. God is at work in us and
his action is always a mystery whose very obscurity leads
us to the truth. It leads us to humility which is an
attitude of truth. We should efface ourselves with a
docility which we feel comes not from ourselves. We
cannot deliberately adopt this attitude. We simply cannot be otherwise in the presence of God. That is why our
attitude is a manifestation of his presence. It is also a
manifestation of what this presence means for us. We
can only be thus in the presence of someone who loves
us infinitely. We should offer our weakness to the omnipotence of grace. We should be poor in a manner that
is itself an act of trust. Our poverty should express our
true attitude to God and show what he means for us.
We are not truly poor unless our awareness of our
poverty profoundly modifies our relations with our
neighbours.

We should humbly accept the feebleness of our prayer
even if we see in it the effect of our own lack of true

detachment and generosity. Allowing the Lord to humiliate us in this way, and gently to accept this humiliation is to open ourselves to grace and to allow it to lead us wherever it wants, for grace sees clearly in our darkness. But true humility prevents us from judging others.

HE IN WHOM WE BELIEVE

Here below progress in the knowledge of God is always a progress in faith. It is not changed into vision. The mystery of God remains far above all our conceptions and we can only stand before it in silence. Faith remains dark and the darkness can even increase. But he who is the object of our faith will appear more and more clearly as the one who means everything to us, the one to whom we surrender in faith with total abandonment.

However the God in whom we believe is not completely unknowable, far off and inaccessible. He is present to us – in our lives – in Christ. He whom our hearts apprehend, and everything in us desires, is not a faceless infinite but someone. Offering the Lord a love which we are no longer even very sure of is to put all our trust in him. When we can only say to God, 'I no longer know whether I love you', this is still a way of telling him that we love him, that we cannot stop loving him. We should offer God our love even if we are not sure that we do love him, gently, peacefully, and show that we really trust him. Before God we can never be humble enough. When we know this we know that we will never fully measure what God is to us and what we can expect from him.

TOTAL TRUST

Let the Lord see that we are prepared to let him do what he likes with us. Our cry to God comes from the depths of our heart and so is part of our simplest self-knowledge. We should learn to recognise it, not try and get it up as if it were not already in us as part of ourselves. We must consent to it. Pay attention to it. Not let ourselves be distracted from it. If our cry to our Father in heaven is in the depths of our heart, this is because we are in living communion with Christ. What is deepest in us only lives in and through this communion, it does not belong to us alone. We should live believing in Christ who lives in us.

If the Lord is really everything to us, this means he must be present in our whole life. We should live this simply trusting in his grace. It is a gift. We must humbly accept it in peace and trust. Our trust leads us towards the mystery of God, leads us to live in its light. Our act of faith brings us a peace which, even if we can hardly feel it, is like no other peace, because it comes from God. We look simply towards God but with our whole being which has become all attention to his presence. When he whom we love is there, even if we do not see him, even if he is silent, his presence clothes our silence. It is not at all like our previous solitude. Our prayer is thus first and foremost the fruit of God's presence. We receive our prayer as a gift, from this presence. We should never doubt his presence. Believing in it is believing in God's love for us. Paying attention to it is letting ourselves be penetrated by its meaning.

In communion with the Lord we live all that we are which is his gift. He is not just someone before whom we stand. He is not just the one we look towards. He is in our looking, in our whole being turned to him. If we were truly open to his grace, if grace could really do what it wanted with us, we would become all love – for God and our neighbour. This would be the surest sign of God's presence. If we see our neighbour as an object of God's love, we will discover that this love is the primary reality, enfolding us and revealing the true meaning of everything else.

HE WHO SPEAKS TO OUR HEART

His love foresees all our needs. It is at work in our hearts far more than we are aware. By its very quietness it forms our attitude of humble acceptance, obedience and respect for its mystery. Everything comes from God, even the response to him which he arouses in our hearts. We must let him form us. We should place no limits on our faith in his love. We should express our faith by a humble acquiescence in what remains mysterious to us. We express our sense of God by clinging to God. This is the deepest movement of our heart, in trust, in obedience. Love. We cannot fathom how it works to accomplish its plan for us. We should not form a purely human idea of its influence. We should not judge it by what we feel or do not feel. We must believe in it with a deep and living faith, not expect to feel it at work. We must simply believe, truly, and not demand signs. We should not have more faith in our weakness than in the fulness of this mystery which is all our hope.

Our weakness is not alone in the presence of this love and unable to respond to it. We are taken hold of by this love, carried by it, united to it in a communion which is a mystery of mercy. We should let this love elicit the consent of our heart, given with our whole freedom.

It is joy to say 'yes' to the Lord, through the power of grace at work in our deepest being. We are aware of it as simply and spontaneously as we are aware of our own existence. Our self-awareness is freed at its deepest level from belonging to itself. We henceforth experience it as a gift, the fruit of God's presence.

The simple and gentle acceptance of knowing we are loved. Our weakness should not make us doubt this love. God loves us because he is love. We are unfailingly sure of him, however silent he may be, however poor and weak we are before him. He is there and that is sufficient. God loves us and we know it. Our peace is very simple but at its heart lies a mystery. Our peace is faith in this mystery. It reveals its hidden presence. The mystery of God's love for us. God gives himself to us by giving us the gift of desiring him. He is at the heart of this desire and reveals himself to us in it. What we believe is a cry to God is already an answer to that cry.

Egoism is unlovable. God only loves in us what is or tries to be open to the love of our neighbour. We should love because God loves, because loving is to be in agreement with God. Everything that we receive from the Lord is given to us in a mystery of communion and thus in openness to other people. We progress together, in a solidarity which is also a mystery beyond our conception. Grace works in us by taking us as we are, in the situation we are in. And we should accept each other just as we are and this is the way to live in communion with each other, in grace.

8

A Mystery of Grace

GOD'S CLOSE PRESENCE

IF GOD'S LOVE is primary, it requires our free consent. But these two realities are not of the same order. Our weakness is not alone in God's sight. It is taken up into the mystery of his infinite love. God's love can discern our free consent however we may express it in our limited way. God's love is at the heart of this consent, it enables us to give it. By giving our consent we should become available to God and dispossessed of self. By giving our consent we should see in other people a mystery of grace demanding our respect. If we go no further than their human weaknesses, this is not seeing other people as they are; they too are taken up into the mystery of the love of God.

God is the one we find beyond ourselves but still in us. We can only reach him by going beyond ourselves, which is the only way of being truly ourselves. God is the Other, because from him we receive everything. But he is not other because we are nothing without him. He is present in our whole being which cannot exist without him. We only exist by the incessant creative power of God. God's creative power is at work in us by nature and by grace. God is always at work in us. When we realise this, it gives our prayer great simplicity and freedom.

We know that our least movement towards God is taken up in the mystery of his fulness, carried by it. We know that we are borne by the goodness of our Father in heaven. He is very close to us. He does not look down on us from the height of heaven. He is with us. That is how we can peacefully live our life as a cry to God, through all our weakness and darkness.

As we become aware of the working of grace, we lose ourselves in it and accept our poverty more simply. We have to accept that all we can offer in reply is faith alone. We are led to it by a deeper sense of the hold this mystery has on our whole being, for it is the mystery of God's love for us. We can put out trust in this love. It is our only hope and no shadow of trust in our own strength should detract from it. To have someone in whom we believe with our whole soul, who is all our hope. That is loving. We should allow grace to deepen our sense of God and make us accept our own humility more peacefully. We should lean inwardly towards a basic obedience, which should become a new mode of existence for us. We should no longer be able to live through any happenings as if they arose from ourselves alone.

THE SECRET LANGUAGE OF OUR HEART

It has been formed slowly in our heart because it has been with us all the days of our life, because he has given us to live with him. His own mark is on us and it cannot be wiped out. It lives in the silence of our heart turned towards God. We must try and hear the secret language of our heart. We must recognise the peace and joy which abide in spite of all our troubles, weakness and anxiety. On the most common occasions when we feel most miserably human, the deep intention of our heart does not change and the Lord sees it even if it is hidden from us. We should accept as a grace of which we are unworthy the ability to offer a prayer like the humblest christian's.

If nothing else, there remains the fact that we cannot do without the Lord. We cannot live without him. We should accept this as a grace and offer it to him as the only thing we have left to offer. We need silence and this is our need for God. If we need silence, this is because we find someone in it. It is more than a desire, it is a concentration in which we are all that we are. It is our very life. We should entrust the Lord with our heart's secret. He alone knows it. At the centre of silence let us find the joy of trusting. A sure trust because God is its support. Our hope need have no limits because it is hope in him who is the negation of limits.

The cry to God in our hearts is a grace, a mystery of grace. It is always deeper than we can fathom. We must believe in this mystery of grace which lives in our hearts. We must silently and humbly hold on to it. We should respect it and pay attention to it. Through the attitudes that grace has formed in us, we can glimpse the mystery of God. We live by grace in the presence of his infinite fulness, and our altered mind can sense it. Our sense of God is our peace, our joy, the reason for our hope. He does not change. He is always with us. God is faithful. He is our refuge. He is our ultimate hope. He will never fail us. We should not be astonished at our poverty in God's sight. Our silence in the presence of his mystery should not lead us to discount everything in us that is a cry to God. We must give our consent to what grace has done in our hearts. We should live with this consent which goes further than we realise. We should allow the Lord to open our hearts to the grace of his presence and make us humbler and more aware of our poverty. As soon as there is the tiniest cry to God in our silence, it is like a small flame which is fed by all the oil that is in the lamp. We should let the Lord choose his own way of showing himself. However quiet it is, let us not be dismayed but live in humble trust.

If we cannot do better, it is that the Lord wants us in this deprived situation. We should not stop believing that we are with him. Putting all our trust in God is having no other reason for hope than the fulness of his love; it is remaining in peace because this hope cannot fail us, however poor and weak we are. We have only to recognise it. As we become more aware of the extent of God's love for us, and his hold on our will and our whole being, our response becomes different, not less but greater. It becomes the expression of a more complete self surrender in perfect trust.

A LISTENING HEART

The incarnation is the divine mystery present in our human condition, accepting the lowliness of our condition for itself. We should not be astonished to have to live the divine mystery in this way. We should recognise its presence in the silence of our hearts, a simple human presence. Only the depths of our heart, its most secret depths can remain truly fixed on God without anything distracting it from him without whom it cannot live. Praying is to discover this in our deepest being and to learn to live with it simply in our poverty. When we have been inattentive or distracted and return to ourselves, do we have the impression that we find our heart again in a conversation with the Lord which he cannot interrupt because he is its very existence?

When the Lord tries us, we can see better how it is he who purifies our heart, forms it by his grace, creates new attitudes in us. This should help us to offer him our silence simply, remembering that he knows what is in our hearts, what he has put in them. He also knows what is still very imperfect in us. Entrusting it to him, is a way, perhaps the truest way of ridding ourselves of it.

We should live in agreement with what God does in us. Our real truth is in belonging to God. We belong to him and he wants to make something of us. He has his plan. The thought that he wants to fulfil this plan in our life in his own way, and that nothing can stop him, should make us accept peacefully everything that comes to us. We should simply entrust ourselves to God's plan for us.

A pure act of faith. But what is the object of our faith? We believe that God loves us, that we are caught up in the grace of his love. If we really believe it we can no longer be the same. We have only to believe strongly enough in the mystery of God's love at work in mankind in all its poverty and sin, in order to see the world and the people round us and our own lives in a quite different way. We respect the mystery and recognise its presence without trying to expose it. We see it as the primary reality which nothing can make us doubt; it is the source of our great hope.

It doesn't matter what we can see or feel, so we should not worry about it. What matters is our attitude, which we may or may not feel all the time, which results simply from paying attention to God's presence, consenting to it. This consent is also a prayer. Consenting to God's presence is agreeing that we depend on it for our very existence. It is agreeing no longer to belong to ourselves. It is an attitude of essential humility. It is also an act of absolute gratitude, believing in God's love for us. Thanksgiving is the proper expression of an act of faith which goes far enough beyond itself to reach the whole of God's love. Thanksgiving knows that it can never go far enough, because it can never measure the love of God. It is in thanksgiving that we can best hold on to all that remains hidden from us. It is sure of God's love. It does not need signs or other reassurances. We should offer our heart to God just as it is, as he sees it with his grace at work in it. Prayer in its many forms is the realisation of belonging to God's love. To God's love for us. Prayer is to be no longer ourselves alone. It is to live in communion. It is to be involved with our whole being in the beyond which this communion opens to us. In this communion our assent to the mystery of God's love for us is taken up into this mystery and becomes a part of it.

A COMMUNION OF FAITH AND LOVE

Perhaps our attitude to God is not visible but we can test it in our behaviour to our neighbour. Our behaviour to them must be governed by our faith in God's presence in them. We have recognised his presence and can never ignore it again. Our apprehension of the mystery of the love of God becomes the core of our attitude to our neighbours. We see that this is the only true response we can make to the mystery. If we are tempted to doubt Christ's presence in ourselves, let us live in an act of faith in his presence in others.

This is a profoundly personal experience, but as we cannot contain the mystery within ourselves alone, our experience needs to be expanded by the faith of others. He towards whom we are moving is he who has spoken to us and whose word we have heard in the communion of believers. We would not move towards him if there was not an impulse in the depths of our hearts, we would not know towards whom we were moving if we had not heard the word. Thus we can follow the movement of our heart quite simply. However obscure it may seem to us, we know where it is leading.

9

The Eyes of Faith

'In this life, faith, as in the next life the light of glory, is the way we see God' (Ascent of Carmel, II 24.).

OUR INMOST SELF

WE MUST LET our heart go its own way, towards its own deepest desire, which it knows is different from all others. This desire is different from all others, not necessarily because it is more strongly felt, but because it comes from further off, from what is deepest in us. It is not simply an act of our free will, but something which is in our deepest being and which involves all that we are. It is something quite simple but inseparable fundamentally from our self-awareness and open to a limitless beyond. God reveals himself to us in this awareness that we are essentially a cry for him.

Our inner atmosphere is not made up only of what we are clearly conscious of and can be precisely expressed. It is also composed of all that is living in our inmost depths. This is what makes us realise what we fundamentally are. It is always there. Let everything within us speak of another and surrender itself to him. A fundamental joy. If we doubt it, we need only ask if we would be prepared to exchange it for any other. We should simply believe in this joy which may be very

secret but which we cannot doubt. We are sure of our
reason for happiness.

A MYSTERY OF GRACE

Everything rests on this mystery which is given to us
to live in faith. It is because we believe in this mystery
that our cry to God, our desire to live by his mystery is
an absolute, a fulness, however feeble our own expression
of it may be. Prayer is not complete in itself. Praying is
to open ourselves. This only makes sense when we believe
in the hidden mystery which requires that we open the
doors of our hearts. Our prayer is secretly taken up in
the grace of God's presence. We would not be surprised
by the obscurity of this presence if we truly believed in
the fulness of its mystery. An inner poverty which is
content to be nothing but hope. Let the depths of our
hearts become all attention.

Believing in God is to offer him in our poverty an act
of faith which can secretly receive from him alone life
and enlightenment. Believing in God is to live with his
presence at the core of our act of faith. Faith is
measured not by the believer but by the object of belief.
In him and through him faith becomes all that it is. He
is present in it. He lives in it and gives it life. Faith is
taken up into his fulness. At the heart of our faith we
already apprehend his presence and know that we should
believe in him totally. Our faith is stronger than all
things because it is of another order.

A CLOSE PRESENCE

Our absolute trust is expressed in absolute simplicity
in our prayer. Putting all our trust in the love of God
is first of all to offer him simply our poor little act of
faith just as it is. The more simply we accept God the
more humbly we trust in him, the closer we feel him
taking hold of us by the grace of his presence. Our faith

is a thin veil which is transparent to the Lord's presence. We know that we receive everything from his presence and this means that the simplest act of faith can open our hearts to him and know that he is close within our reach. In this knowledge we can live with his presence, joyfully, through all the silences. Nothing can stop us believing in it, expecting everything from it, because our faith and hope rely on it. Our faith may seem a little thing to us. We do not put our trust in our own faith, but in God in whom we believe. The humbler our faith, the truer it is.

Christ is always with us. His presence and atmosphere is the continuity of our prayer through all the acts of faith which renew our contact with him. We have a relationship by faith with Christ who identifies with us. This relationship is at the centre of what is most personal in us. We should turn every difficulty into an increase of trust. Believing in God means knowing that we can never trust him too much. We should entrust ourselves to God's love which he has for us personally. We should learn to discern his presence in our lives.

Even when we no longer know it, can no longer say we believe it, God loves us and keeps us in his hands. The Lord sees our hearts, our true deep desires. He sees us already as what we should like to be. His grace is always active, freely going before. If it meets with obstacles in us this does not hinder it. It only asks us to allow these obstacles to give way bit by bit, to let it work. It will gradually make our hearts gentler and more peaceful. Grace alone can do this.

THE FREEDOM OF LOVE

Faith gives us a glimpse of God's fulness of charity for all things. People who hurt us and, we feel, do us wrong are also in this order and harmony of charity. God knows his secret ways. We should have enough faith in

God's love to follow him peacefully along his own ways.
This is the freedom of entrusting everything to the Lord
and putting all our trust in him. It is a freedom lived
in gratitude. We should look at things simply, that is to
say freed from all the complications of self-attachment.

We apprehend the fulness of God's love as a mystery
in which we are involved, which lives in us. Let us also
recognise it in our neighbours. We should at least respect
our neighbour's secret self in the eyes of God. We
should try not to look at him with our eyes alone. There
is always a beyond which eludes us. A beyond where a
person's deepest truth only exists in God's sight. We
receive everything from God's love in the communion
with him he has granted us. In him may we become
nothing but love. Let us become incapable of not loving.

ALIVE WITH CHRIST

We tremble before the mystery. We hardly dare credit
the fulness of communion in which Christ in his all
prevailing love has made us so truly at one with himself. In the ever present grace of his Eucharist where
we get an inkling of the mystery, we are completely
united with him. In us he lives his sonship to the Father.
We enter into it with him, in him. Prayer cannot be
thought of as a precise operation which can be rigor-
ously defined. Prayer is being ready and open for an
unforeseeable exchange, a lived communion in which we
gradually discover the Other by learning to be truly ourselves in his presence. We should live in freedom what
God's ever present love brings to life in our hearts. We
receive it from God. Let us receive it in simple trust. Let
us acquiesce. Give our consent. Let our consent pay
attention.

Let us believe in God's love, in his faithfulness. He is
always at work in our hearts, making our prayer fruitful by taking it up into his fulness. He turns it into a

mystery which goes beyond us and whose secret we must respect. We can be certain that our faintest cry opens our heart to God's love. May the simplicity of our hope bear witness to him in whom we have put our trust. A simplicity which is confidence. Let us simply keep close to him who is our only hope. We need nothing but his presence. The presence of the Lord apprehended by perfect trust. He is the one who cannot fail us. The fulness of the mystery in which our hope rests, recognised by the very simplicity of our trust. The way we trust him expresses what we have glimpsed of his fulness. A silence filled with the sense of God's infinite fulness, infinitely beyond us but also infinitely close.

Let us really look to the Lord, to him alone. Let our prayer be a total act of faith in his active presence whose grace takes hold of every heart that really desires it, however poor and weak that heart may feel. Let us be completely docile, at the Lord's disposal and he will see our hearts.

Praying is being open to God's mystery, being taken up into this mystery. It is to enter into a communion with an infinite which wants to come close to us. We cannot see God but we can welcome the gift of his presence. We can pay attention to this presence. His presence begins our awareness and opens the way to his love. And we know that it remains even when we cannot feel it. In dark times we could have doubts about what is in our hearts, if what was there belonged to us alone. But what is in our hearts comes from beyond us. God gives it life and him we cannot doubt. We are sure of his love's faithfulness whose ultimate expression is his mercy. Doubting our own love in dark and difficult times would be to doubt God's love for us. We should pray with confident abandonment and also live.

Conclusion

QUITE SIMPLY LET our behaviour conform with our deepest truth, with what we are. Let it express our awareness that we are children of God. Our self awareness is then bound to be a prayer. We only have a full awareness of what we are in prayer. Praying is being. It is not something added on, it is being aware of what we are. It is and remains our deepest truth even when we walk in darkness.[1]

1. Prayer, in the full sense can only be addressed to God. It is an attitude appropriate only before God. This should have been made clear by all that we have said above. What we call prayer to the saints – perhaps to call it recourse to their intercession – poses an ecumenical problem which appears to us to be a problem not about prayer, but about the communion of saints. That is why we have not discussed it. What we wish to stress here is that prayer, in the strong sense, can only be addresses to God. Catholic theology makes this plain by using two different words for worship of God and honour of the saints.